Released To Rebuild

Meditations For People
Released From Bondage
To Rebuild Their Lives

David Lowry

HopeAbides

Released To Rebuild
Meditations For People Released From Bondage To Rebuild Their Lives
Copyright © 2012 by David Lowry

Contents

Contents

Introduction

By the rivers of Babylon—there we sat down
>and there we wept when we remembered
>>Zion.
On the willows there
>we hung up our harps.
For there our captors
>asked us for songs,
and our tormentors asked for mirth,
>saying, "Sing us one of the songs of Zion!"
How could we sing the Lord's song
>in a foreign land?
If I forget you, O Jerusalem,
>let my right hand wither!
Let my tongue cling to the roof of my mouth,
>if I do not remember you,
if I do not set Jerusalem
>above my highest joy. (Psalm 137:1-6)

In 586 BC, the Babylonians destroyed Jerusalem and the temple. That which was at the center of Jewish life and identity was razed to the ground. City and temple were turned to rubble. The people of Jerusalem and the surrounding area were taken captive and brought to Babylon where they remained in captivity for seventy years. At the end of seventy years, the people of Israel were allowed to go back to their homeland where they rebuilt their homes, the city wall and temple. In the books of Ezra and Nehemiah, we are given the story of their return and rebuilding. We are told that, at times, they had to build the city wall while under attack by those who sought their defeat.

Leading up to their exile and during their captivity, there were prophets who declared God's action in these events. Because of their idolatry, God brought judgment upon the people of Israel through the Babylonians. God sat them down in Babylon to break their false dependencies. God spoke to them there, and God opened the way for their return. God called them to rebuild and God was with them in their rebuilding.

This pattern of captivity, freedom and rebuilding depicts our lives as well. We are bound by addictions, obsessions and idolatries. That to which we can be addicted goes far beyond drugs as demonstrated by the proliferation of twelve step programs. There are groups for overeaters, gamblers, gamers, debtors, workaholics, shoppers, spenders, clutterers, sex and love addicts and survivors of incest. There are Social Phobics Anonymous, Depressed Anonymous, Emotions Anonymous, Schizophrenia Anonymous, Vulgarity Anonymous, and for those who have gotten addicted to their support group, there is Anonymity Anonymous.

We can be addicted not only to various activities, but also to emotions and attitudes. We can be attached to our fear, anxiety, anger, bitterness or need for control. We can continually be seeking for a particular feeling that we think we cannot live without. We can even be addicted to a particular image of ourselves that always has to be defended. We may be afraid of the true self God would have us become, because we are so stuck on the one we imagine.

Above all, sin holds us captive. "We are in bondage to sin and cannot free ourselves," as a prayer of confession puts it. We serve idols. We worship money, power, status, pleasure, comfort and convenience. Add your own idol to the list. Of course, it is always power or status or pleasure for ourselves that we serve and worship. We are our own best idol. We have national and societal idols as well: nationalism, racism, classism, militarism, consumerism, etc. Whatever the idol, it holds us captive and keeps us from our true selves which are found in God. We have been alienated and cut off from our source, living in bondage to that for which we were not created. Our idolatry demeans us. It forms the spiritual roots of injustice, oppression, breakdown and division. Furthermore, our worship of the creature rather than the creator cannot be prevented. We are bound. When we begin to get honest about this situation, we ask, "Who can set us free from this bondage to sin and spiritual death?"

With God there is deliverance. "In Christ God was reconciling the world to himself (2 Corinthians 5:19)." God was bringing us back to himself through Jesus Christ who died on a cross and was raised from the dead. Our way back from exile has been provided for us. Through Jesus Christ, we are able to "turn to God from idols, to serve a living and true God" (1 Thessalonians 1:9). We are being released from bondage to idolatry.

We are also discovering that this being set free has put us on a journey. Being released from bondage, we now have the work of rebuilding our lives. We are seeking to grow in the new life that God has for us in Jesus Christ. We are rebuilding our relationships and households. We are learning to let God enter into every area of our lives and make the changes that must be made.

Just as God brought Israel back from exile and called it to rebuild, so God calls us. The following pages focus on the theme of release and rebuilding through a series of meditations on scripture. We start with the reality of God bringing us back to himself through Jesus Christ. It is God who does the work of releasing us. It is God who helps us to acknowledge that we are in bondage and need help. It is God who empowers us for rebuilding.

Released From Bondage

1 It Is All God!

When Israel was a child, I loved him,
    and out of Egypt I called my son.
The more I called them,
    the more they went from me;
they kept sacrificing to the Baals,
    and offering incense to idols.
Yet it was I who taught Ephraim to walk,
    I took them up in my arms;
but they did not know
    that I healed them.
I led them with cords of human kindness,
    with bands of love.
I was to them like those who lift infants to
        their cheeks.
    I bent down to them and fed them.
They shall return to the land of Egypt, and
        Assyria shall be their king,
    because they have refused to return to me.
The sword rages in their cities, it consumes
        their oracle-priests,
    and devours because of their schemes.
My people are bent on turning away from me.
    To the Most High they call, but he does not
        raise them up at all.
How can I give you up, Ephraim?
    How can I hand you over, O Israel?
How can I make you like Admah?
    How can I treat you like Zeboiim?

My heart recoils within me;
>   my compassion grows warm and tender.
I will not execute my fierce anger;
>   I will not again destroy Ephraim;
for I am God and no mortal, the Holy One in
>   your midst,
>   and I will not come in wrath.
They shall go after the LORD, who roars like a
>   lion;
>   when he roars, his children shall come trem-
>   bling from the west.
They shall come trembling like birds from
>   Egypt,
>   and like doves from the land of Assyria;
>   and I will return them to their homes,
>   says the LORD. (Hosea 11:1-11)

God is the initiator and actor in bringing his people back to himself. It is not so much about us, but about God. It is always God who takes care of us! It is God who lets us run away from him! It is God who brings us back! Every good and perfect gift comes from God—even the gifts that don't look like gifts!

It is always God who takes care of us!

God tells us that he has always loved us. God loves us when we are in a trusting relationship with him, and God loves us when we are far away from him. The Bible tells us that God grieves when we turn away from him, and does not stop loving us. God hurts because he loves us. We hear the hurt in the word of the Lord that comes through Hosea: "The more I called them, the more they went from me." That sounds like grief.

Like Israel, we have gone after idols of our own imaginations. We have lived for our own pleasure and comfort and convenience. We have sacrificed our lives for money, power and prestige. It must hurt God when we act as if money got us out of the jam we were in. It must hurt God when we sacrifice for the sake of the god of money and then believe it paid off. We believe it bought our way out of some problem, and we give praise to it. It must hurt God when we give homage to the information god, and we think that our education saved us—and that it will save others as well. As if our smarts get us out of trouble.

It must hurt God when we idolize power and offer sacrifices in the way of flattery or subservience to the well connected, and think we were saved out of our problems by connections. It must hurt God when we give all praise to the glories of technology, when some medical breakthrough has helped us with our healing. We act like the God who created our bodies and minds is not even present. We give all praise to human ingenuity. It must hurt God from whom every good and perfect gift comes.

Martin Luther, in his explanation of the first commandment, "Thou shalt have no other gods before me," writes that God is saying to us, "See to it that you let Me alone be your God, and never seek another....Whatever you lack of good things, expect it of Me, and look to Me for it, and whenever you suffer misfortune and distress, come and cling to Me. I, yes, I, will give you enough and help you out of every need; only let not your heart cleave to or rest in any other" (Martin Luther, *Large Catechism*).

We have a problem with our hearts cleaving and resting in the wrong center—in people, places and things. We have a problem with our hearts drawing away from God. There is an old hymn, "Come, Thou Fount of Every Blessing" with a verse that speaks to our wandering hearts:

> O to grace how great a debtor
> > Daily I'm constrained to be!
> Let Thy goodness, like a fetter,
> > Bind my wandering heart to Thee.
> Prone to wander, Lord, I feel it,
> > Prone to leave the God I love;
> Here's my heart, O take and seal it,
> > Seal it for Thy courts above.

Our hearts do tend to wander, and we tend to give thanks and praise to the idols of our culture and society. We incline toward pride in what our money does for us or our smarts or schemes or plans or great advice.

To this, God says, "It was I who taught [you all] to walk, I took [you] up in my arms; but [you] did not know that I healed [you]." (Children do not generally know what their parents go through for them or how their parents are watching over them even when they are misbehaving.) God watches out for us, even when we wander from him.

It is always God who takes care of us whether we are near to God or far! He makes the rain fall and the sun shine on saint and sinner alike. If we have been cared for, it has always been God. If we have been healed, it has been God. If we have a job today, it is God. If we have food on the table today, it is God. If we got through that exam or trial or tribulation, it was God. We may have put the credit somewhere else, but it was God! God created and gifted us. Jesus tells us that our Father in heaven makes it rain on the just and the unjust. To both sinners and the righteous, God gives what is needed for their crops to grow.

We may talk about how smart we are or show off what money has brought us or pride ourselves for some victory. But the truth is, every good and perfect gift comes from God. It is God who watches over us. When we are running away from him, he is still taking care of us, giving us a little more time to turn back to him.

When we realize this, we have to start thanking God. I need to thank God for all those times he took care of me when I did not have the sense to thank him. Even now God is giving to us freely in order that our needs might be met.

"Thank you Lord! Thank you for food on my table and shelter from the elements. Thank you for the people you put into my life. Thank you for strength to make it through the hard times and to embrace another day and realize it is a new day. Thank you for hope and faith and love."

"Even so, I am 'prone to wander, Lord, I feel it, prone to leave the God I love.' And sometimes when I wander, you let me go." The God who cares for me is also the God who lets me run away from him—if I am so willful and determined.

It is God who lets us run away from him!

God, at times, lets us run away and yet still loves us even while he is letting us go. When God's people "are bent on turning away from [him]," he will say, "They shall return to bondage, and be ruled over, because they have refused to return to me. They will experience the consequences of their going away from me, in the destruction in their cities, and the downfall of the proponents of their idols. And this destruction will come because of their schemes and plans."

The God who is love, created creatures who are able to love, and therefore who are also able to refuse to love. (We know that love is not love unless freely given.) And God honors his creatures who have the capacity to love or not to love by letting them choose. What do you do when someone rejects you? You have to let that person go.

There is no good in trying to force yourself on someone who will not have you.

God respects us as the free creatures he created. He lets us go, if we will not have him! He loves us by letting us go. He knows that outside of him there is only bondage. He knows that when we turn from him, we turn back to bondage. He knows that our plans and schemes take us back into captivity. And he lets us go, and waits.

Sometimes, as parents, we will let our children experience the consequences of their decisions. We will counsel them about a decision but let them make up their own minds. We will do this in different ways at different ages. When my children were teenagers, they had more freedom than when they were younger, and within certain boundaries they could make decisions I did not agree with. Now that they are young adults, their decisions are their own. I have to let them go.

God, at times, lets us go. God does not let us go easily, however. For new Christians, babes in Christ, God is very protective. He gives them the experience of new life. He gives them the fellowship of other believers. He gives them the Holy Spirit. He provides helps and boundaries, Bible studies and the word and prayer. But there does come a time, when they have to venture forth in faith and take new steps and make new decisions. They have to grow up in Christ. They have to take the risk of faith. They have to make decisions to die to the old, to let go, to come out of something they have been into that is not of the Lord. They have to take steps.

And they feel the risk of taking new steps. They realize that they can turn back to the old comfort zones and the old ways. They are tempted. They may think to themselves, "I have spent years building up a life for myself that I got used to, and I don't know that I want to give it all up. Couldn't I go back to some things and just take God with me? Maybe I will still do some things that God doesn't really have for me but keep him around to bless those things I like."

They may even start to feel the power they have in being able to decide about their lives and make much of this power. They talk about their freedom to do what they want, and they say that that doesn't mean they will not still pray and think about God. They are now rationalizing their decisions and going backwards and returning to former bondages. And God lets go. He says, "You shall return to bondage—until you learn what your plans and schemes are truly doing to you."

God, in his love for us, will let us get to a place of pain and confusion until we have had enough and will reach out to him again. God is at work when he is dealing with wayward children by letting them go.

It is God who brings us back!

Even when we are reaching out for God from the place of pain and confusion, it is God who is bringing us back to himself. He is "like a lion to his cubs. He roars and they come home trembling." And he reestablishes them.

God calls us back to himself through his word. He calls us back and draws our hearts to himself, and releases us from bondage so that we can rebuild our lives in him! Has God been calling you back from some place today? Has he been trying to bring you back to himself? God does not want us to stay on a road that leads to destruction.

Maybe you chose a road he did not have for you to take. Perhaps you got into a relationship he did not have for you, or a situation or scheme that did not come from him. Maybe you even dressed it up spiritually—the thing you got caught up in—with a "spiritual" rationalization. But in your heart of hearts, you feel that it is not really, truly right. God is working on your heart. God is calling you back to himself, to receive from him what he has for you.

We do not need to make up God's plan for us. He will give us what we truly need. Our loving Father will give us good and perfect gifts. God has what we need today.

2 Admitting We Are Bound

Thus says the LORD: Cursed are those who trust in mere mortals and make mere flesh their strength, whose hearts turn away from the LORD. They shall be like a shrub in the desert, and shall not see when relief comes. They shall live in the parched places of the wilderness, in an uninhabited salt land. Blessed are those who trust in the LORD, whose trust is the LORD. They shall be like a tree planted by water, sending out its roots by the stream. It shall not fear when heat comes, and its leaves shall stay green; in the year of drought it is not anxious, and it does not cease to bear fruit. The heart is devious above all else; it is perverse—who can understand it? I the LORD test the mind and search the heart, to give to all according to their ways, according to the fruit of their doings. (Jeremiah 17:5-10)

God's Word makes it clear: We are under a curse when we trust in ourselves. We are blessed when we trust in the Lord. Those who trust in themselves are like a shrub in the desert. Even when relief comes they will pass it up because they will not even be able to discern that it is relief.

On the other hand, those who trust in the Lord, whose trust is the Lord, they will be like a tree planted by water, "sending out its roots by the stream. It shall not fear when heat comes, and its leaves shall stay green; in the year of drought it is not anxious, and it does not cease to bear fruit." Those whose trust is in the Lord are anchored in the Lord and therefore, when they are going through the time of trial, they are still being blessed and bearing fruit. They are not anxious because their lives are in God's hands.

Jeremiah speaks these wonderful words that he received from the Lord, and we all nod our heads and think how great it is for us, if we simply trust in the Lord and not lean unto our own understanding. If we would live each day completely trusting God, there would be nothing but blessing even in the hard times. We want it, and we reach out for it. We tell ourselves that we are going to trust in the Lord because there is great blessing in the Lord. And we make a commitment to ourselves that this week, we are going to go through the week trusting in the Lord. This is the desire of our hearts, and we want the blessing that will come with trusting.

But then—just as we are making this commitment in our hearts—Jeremiah says something that is so very sobering: "The heart is devious above all else; it is perverse—who can understand it?" Or as the King James Version has it: "The heart is deceitful above all things, and desperately wicked—who can know it?" John Wesley had his way of saying it:

> There is nothing so false and deceitful as the heart of man; deceitful in its apprehensions of things, in the hopes and promises which it nourishes, in the assurances that it gives us; unsearchable by others, deceitful with reference to ourselves, and abominably wicked, so that neither can a man know his own heart, nor can any other know that of his neighbor's. (*John Wesley's Notes*)

Carl Jung, the famous Swiss psychoanalyst who spent many years counseling troubled individuals, wrote in his mid-eighties that when you pull back layer after layer of defenses and walls of repression what you find is evil of gigantic proportions. "The heart is deceitful above all things, and desperately wicked—who can know it?"

Why is the heart desperately wicked? Because it trusts in itself. It is stuck on itself. Martin Luther (following St. Augustine) defined sin as our "being turned in on ourselves." In the depths of our being, we are turned inward to worship ourselves rather than the creator. Our very hearts are misdirected, and what flows from our hearts is the same.

Our hearts are desperately wicked not because we think and do bad things. We think and do bad things because our hearts are desperately wicked. We think and act selfishly, pridefully and self-servingly because our hearts—rather than being centered in God—are centered in themselves. The cause of breakdown in our relationships, our tensions with one another, our trying to prove ourselves to others, our fighting over position and recognition, our gossip, our slander, our stinginess, greed, jealousy, envy, spiteful ways, unkind and cruel words, thoughtless words and actions—all of this comes from our hearts that are turned in on themselves.

Jeremiah is saying something about all of us including himself: Our hearts are desperately wicked, and they are *deceitful* above all things. Our desperately wicked hearts lie. They lie to themselves. We lie to ourselves. We do it unconsciously as a matter of habit. For this reason, those involved in spiritual counseling or prayer for inner healing end up pulling back layers of denial or getting beneath symptoms to root causes. What we give as the reason for our dysfunctional actions, is rarely the true reason. The truth is we do not know why we do many of the things we do, because we have done such a good job at lying to ourselves. Our hearts are deceitful above all things.

What is to be done for us in such a state? We cannot even discern our own thoughts. In the deceitfulness of our hearts we can, with great ease, talk about how discerning we are, when the truth is we are blind. Even as Christians who are committed to following Jesus and care about the truth, we will often, in our pride, think more highly of ourselves then we ought when it comes to spiritual discernment. In the deceitfulness of our hearts and from a place of pride, we will ascribe to the Holy Spirit all kinds of things that are not holy. And we will give our reasons, strange reasons: "I know it was from the Lord because the thought was so sudden." "I know it was from the Lord because it lined up with something else in my life, and it couldn't be just a coincidence." "It must be from the Lord because I feel so strongly about it."

The heart is exceedingly deceitful! It makes up good reasons for bad ideas. There are so many hidden causes for the things we say and do—feelings, attitudes, lusts, biases, prejudices, pride, hankerings after this or that, desire to please others and concerns about what we are going to get out of something. Much that is unexamined in our hearts gives rise to all kinds of thoughts, words and actions.

Who can save us out of this vicious cycle of lies and deceit? "I the LORD test the mind and search the heart, to give to all according to their ways, according to the fruit of their doings." God knows us. God knows from whence our thoughts and actions arise. We need the Lord who tests the mind and searches the heart. We cannot save ourselves from this situation of deceit. We need the Lord every day because of the state of our hearts. Left to ourselves we are hedged in by our deceitful ways.

We need a Savior. We cannot trust our own hearts. We cannot trust the commitments our hearts make. We cannot trust that our hearts will carry out the commitments just because our hearts have told us how earnest they are. Our hearts are desperately wicked and deceitful. And we do not even know our own hearts. We do not know ourselves. Our lives have become unmanageable, and we cannot save ourselves.

Paul says: "I know that nothing good dwells within me, that is, in my flesh. I can will what is right, but I cannot do it. For I do not do the good I want, but the evil I do not want is what I do. Now if I do what I do not want, it is no longer I that do it, but sin that dwells within me" (Romans 7:18). It sounds like Paul is saying, "My life has become unmanageable and I cannot save myself." He then says: "Wretched man that I am! Who will rescue me from this body of death? Thanks be to God through Jesus Christ our Lord" (Romans 7:24)!

What we have been unable to do for ourselves, God has done for us through Jesus Christ who died and was raised for us. Come to the Savior today. Receive from the Savior today. Where else are we to go? He has the words of life! God comes to establish a relationship with us and to do for us what we have been unable to do for ourselves. It is not about trying harder to fix our lives, but it is about our coming, in our desperate need, to God our Savior who alone can save us.

I once got a card from my daughter that on the outside read, "Dad, I love listening to your advice." On the inside it said, "Not that I follow it, but you have a very pleasant speaking voice." This is the way it is, at times, with us. There are things that we read in the Bible or hear in a hymn or gospel song that touch us. It seems to us that God has a pleasant speaking voice. We may make it to church to hear that voice again and again, hoping that we will feel a little better when we leave so that we can make it through another week. But not much changes in our week.

Have you been spending time listening to the voice without following it? The point at which our lives change, is that point where we start trusting. God is at work in us to bring us to the place where we have made up our minds, so that we now say from our hearts, "I will trust in the Lord until I die."

There was a rich man who ran up to Jesus and asked him how he could have eternal life. He told Jesus that he had been keeping the commandments since his youth. (You shall not murder; You shall not commit adultery; You shall not steal; You shall not bear false witness; You shall not defraud; Honor your father and mother.) "Jesus, looking at him, loved him and said, 'You lack one thing; go, sell what you own, and give the money to the poor, and you will have treasure in heaven; then come, follow me'" (Mark 10:21).

Before this man could follow Jesus, he had to let go of what he had been trusting in. The one thing that was getting in the way of this man following Jesus was his riches. His riches were more important to him, even if following Jesus meant eternal life. We know that because it says: "When he heard this, he was shocked and went away grieving, for he had many possessions."

God knows our hearts. He knows what our hearts lean on and trust in, and he will go right at that which keeps us from trusting in him and following Jesus. He will go right at that relationship or reality that we have refused to give up because it is where our hearts are centered. In the deceitfulness of our hearts, we have tried to tell ourselves that we could have God's life and hold onto our idol as well. But Jesus comes to us and speaks God's word right to that which we have lived for and trusted in. He says, "Give it up. Let it go. And then come follow me."

God has come to us in Jesus Christ to release us from bondage in order that we might rebuild our lives. Before we can rebuild our lives we have to be released from trusting in that which we have made an idol. Before we can begin to rebuild our lives we have to place our trust in the Lord.

God reveals to us what we cling to. What is God showing you today? Is he showing you something right now that he is calling you to let go of? You do not have to go away sad like the rich young man, still holding onto something that has not blessed you because it could not bless you. Only God can bless you.

What has been impossible for you, is possible with God. In Christ Jesus, he has done for you what you could not do for yourself. Jesus lived by complete trust in his Father in heaven, so that through him you might also live by trust, forsaking all others for the sake of the kingdom.

Jesus stands before you calling you to trust. Calling you to "let go and let God." He says, "Make up your mind." "You cannot serve two masters." He also says, "See, I am helping you. I am releasing you. Therefore, let go. Let go right now. Fight me no longer. Surrender to me, for I am Lord."

Make up your mind and pray: "I will trust in the Lord. I will trust in the Lord until I die."

3 Two Kinds Of Temptation

> But now thus says the LORD, he who created you, O Jacob, he who formed you, O Israel: Do not fear, for I have redeemed you; I have called you by name, you are mine. When you pass through the waters, I will be with you; and through the rivers, they shall not overwhelm you; when you walk through fire you shall not be burned, and the flame shall not consume you. For I am the LORD your God, the Holy One of Israel, your Savior. (Isaiah 43:1-3)

This word comes to a people in captivity. It comes with the promise of deliverance. This people will be released from bondage to rebuild their lives. This promise comes from the one who created and formed them and who calls them by name. This message of salvation comes with great encouragement: "Do not fear!" And it speaks the future as if it were present: "I have redeemed you." In other words, you may not be experiencing your release from captivity right at this moment, but know that it has already been accomplished. It is now time for you to walk into it!

Walking into your freedom demands steps that must be taken. Being released from captivity means going through trial. But you will endure. "When you pass through the waters, I will be with you; and through the rivers, they shall not overwhelm you; when you walk through fire you shall not be burned, and the flame shall not consume you. For I am the LORD your God, the Holy One of Israel, your Savior."

You are going to endure hardships on your way home, and you are going to face problems when you get home. When you arrive home, you are going to have to rebuild. Many of us have been rescued out of a mess that is, in part, of our own making. And now that we are being set free from that which we were caught up in and which others in our lives had a share in, we have to go back and face the disorder. But now we face it with a new mind and a freed mind. God is saying to us, "I release you from bondage so that you can rebuild your life. Therefore, go back to your home and your situations and do the rebuilding that I have for you to do."

Some people never get to the place of rebuilding their lives. On their way from captivity to the promised land, they get bogged down in the wilderness. They start complaining about the journey or remember what they have left behind. What they have left has an addictive power; they still think they *need* it. They forget that deliverance from bondage means going home to our true selves and to God's purposes and presence. There are trials and temptations associated with going home.

Consider the Israelites returning from bondage in Babylon to Judah and Jerusalem. They faced dangers on the return journey, as they traveled through the wilderness. On their five hundred mile trek from Babylon to Jerusalem, they contended with wild animals and exposure to the elements. They crossed rivers and endured storms, lightening and fires. They faced storms—water and fire! Water overwhelms and fire overtakes.

When released from bondage—whatever our bondage has been—we can expect to face impediments on our way to rebuilding our lives. The words of St. Paul speak to this situation: "For freedom Christ has set us free. Stand firm, therefore, and do not submit again to a yoke of slavery" (Galatians 5:1). You have been released in order to rebuild.

Stand firm therefore. Do not turn back! As in the words of a song, "I have decided to follow Jesus, no turning back, no turning back. The cross before me, the world behind me, no turning back."

What would take us back? What are we up against on this journey of freedom? Being set free to rebuild our lives, what would prevent us? What would cause us to turn back? Consider two kinds of temptation that we face, as we move back to the situations of our lives to rebuild. One is like water; the other is like fire.

"When you pass through the waters, I will be with you; and through the rivers, they shall not overwhelm you; when you walk through fire you shall not be burned, and the flame shall not consume you." We will pass through the waters and we will walk through fire. We will have to deal with temptations that can either overwhelm us or overtake us. One temptation is like water, subtle and incessant. It can overwhelm us. The other is like fire. It involves the trials that can overtake us.

Temptation like water—subtle and incessant.

Some temptations are like rising floods. The rain keeps coming down, and the rivers swell, and the flood waters rise until they are finally over our heads. These temptations are subtle and incessant. They keep coming, and they keep undermining our faith. They may seem at first to be a drizzle of water, but they eventually become a torrent. Little by little they take us away from our journey of faith. They take us away from following Jesus. Subtly and incessantly they pry us away from our first love. Little by little they displace Jesus with a lot of other concerns.

"One is tempted by one's own desire, being lured and enticed by it; then, when that desire has conceived, it gives birth to sin, and that sin, when it is fully grown, gives birth

21

to death" (James 1:14-15). The old life outside of Christ is a life that we lived by our desires and our lusts. We lived by their enticement and thought nothing of it. What was conceived was sin, and sin was habitual. It was mostly all we knew. But now that we have come to Christ Jesus and been born anew into a new life, we find that there is a struggle. When we were doing what the power of evil had for us to do, we didn't know that it was like a roaring lion seeking to devour. We were already being devoured and did not have enough sense to know it. But now, with the Holy Spirit in our lives, we are seeing it today. We are in a battle, and it is a battle for our lives. It is a battle between the old life that remains near and the new life in Christ.

Augustine, the African bishop of the fifth century, shared his own experience as a new Christian:

> As yet I was bound by the iron chain of my own will. The enemy held fast my will, and had made of it a chain, and had bound me tight with it. For out of the perverse will came lust, and the service of lust ended in habit, and habit, not resisted, became necessity. By these links, as it were, forged together—which is why I called it "a chain"—a hard bondage held me in slavery. But that new will which had begun to spring up in me freely to worship thee and to enjoy thee, O my God, the only certain Joy, was not able as yet to overcome my former willfulness, made strong by long indulgence. Thus my two wills—the old and the new, the carnal and the spiritual—were in conflict within me; and by their discord they tore my soul apart.

Maybe you feel that is you today. There is a new life you are beginning to experience in Christ, but the old seems very alive. In your mind, you want to do God's will, but it seems there is something that is working against it, and it has you bound because you do the very thing that you do not want to do. It is the sin in you.

We *feel* so vulnerable to temptation because, left to ourselves, we *are* vulnerable. We can come to a service of worship and experience joy and peace in the Lord, walk out of church, and before we get home, evil words come out of our mouths that we thought we left behind. We react to something our child or our spouse is doing and express attitudes that do not fit with the worship experience we just shared.

There is a temptation that is like water. It is subtle and incessant. It keeps rising so that it might finally overwhelm us like a rising flood. It works on our desires, our pride, our fears. It grabs at us and inserts itself to take hold of us and have us doing what it bids us do.

It is subtle. It can come in religious guise. That is why we are cautioned about a religion that has become a matter of form rather than the source of power and life. This is the danger especially for those active in church. We are tempted to think that being at church and doing church work is the main thing. We get good at church activities, and those activities come to displace the thing that is most important—our relationship with the Lord and our following him. That is why Jesus said to his followers: "Do not rejoice at this, that the spirits submit to you, but rejoice that your names are written in heaven" (Luke 10:20). Rejoice in your relationship with God.

The danger of this subtle and incessant temptation is that it sneaks up on us. It will overwhelm us before we know it. We start to give in a little here and a little there, and before we realize it, we are back in captivity. Our only hope is in the Lord. It is certainly not in ourselves. "When you pass through the waters, I will be with you; and through the rivers, they shall not overwhelm you." God promises to be with us through the trials and temptations. In him, we are more than conquerors.

Temptation like fire—coming with trials and tribulations.

Do you find that you get overtaken by trials and tribulations? When a trial comes, you forget God. You are taken out by it. You cannot even make it to the gathered community of God's people. You have trouble praying and spending time in God's presence. You are too caught up in anxiety, trying to maintain control and hold things together, to take time with the Lord. You have been overtaken.

I grew up in southern California where Santa Anna winds could blow a fire into an extremely dangerous inferno. Just as it is virtually impossible to outrun a fire being blown by a 50 mile an hour wind, left to ourselves we cannot outrun the trials and tribulations when they come. We will have to walk through them. Our hope is in the Lord's presence with us: "When you walk through fire you shall not be burned, and the flame shall not consume you." Trials come with the opportunity to grow in faith and in the Lord. In such times, if we will trust in the Lord, we will come out stronger in the Lord. The temptation in each trial, however, is to escape not to the living God but to something else—for some, drugs and alcohol; for others, isolation; for still others, it will be partying, as if all I need do is turn up the volume of my life and drown out the trial.

God wants us to trust him at such times. These are times to put our complete trust in him. If we do so, he will lift us up. God will reveal ways of life we could not have seen otherwise. He will teach us. He will instruct us in our hearts. He will heal us and restore us through such times.

He will do a new work in us. "When you pass through the waters, I will be with you; and through the rivers, they shall not overwhelm you; when you walk through fire you shall not be burned, and the flame shall not consume you. For I am the LORD your God, the Holy One of Israel, your Savior." God is our Savior. We find salvation no where else.

Before the Risen Jesus ascended into heaven, he told his followers what they were to do. His instructions provide direction for what to do when suddenly we feel Jesus' absence. It is good advice when we are being tempted, when all kinds of trials and temptations are coming our way, when the "devil is like a roaring lion" and God seems far away and the old life and ways so very near (1 Peter 5:8). "Jesus ordered them not to leave Jerusalem, but to wait there for the promise of the Father. 'This,' he said, 'is what you have heard from me; for John baptized with water, but you will be baptized with the Holy Spirit'" (Acts 1:4-5). And then, "You will receive power when the Holy Spirit has come upon you; and you will be my witnesses in Jerusalem, in all Judea and Samaria, and to the ends of the earth" (Acts 1:8).

When you and I are facing trials and temptations, it is time to wait for what the Father promises us. What we need is the power of the Holy Spirit. And we do not get that power out in the world with our old ways of operating, isolated from the community of faith. We need to do like those first followers. We need to come together and lift our hands and hearts upward, stretching out for God's help and power.

Will you do that right now? Whatever you are going through, whatever you are facing, there is power for you from on high. The Lord has promised not to leave you or forsake you. The power of evil would tempt you not to believe that. It would tempt you to believe that the

Holy Spirit is not near or is not there for you. The devil would have you look to someone else. This word is for us: Wait for the promise of the Father. Your father in heaven promises to immerse you in the Holy Spirit. He has power for you right now today! He will turn you from the fear of things that have been coming against you and make you witnesses to the ends of the earth.

When Jesus "had been baptized and was praying, the heaven was opened, and the Holy Spirit descended upon him in bodily form like a dove. And a voice came from heaven, 'You are my Son, the Beloved; with you I am well pleased'" (Luke 3:21-22). What our Father in heaven did for Jesus, he chooses to do for us because of Jesus and through him. He pours out upon us his Holy Spirit, and he says to us, "You are my child, my beloved." Let him do that for you today. You belong to him, and he gives you what you need to overcome those things that used to overpower you.

4 Where Faith Begins

Then the word of the LORD came to him, saying, "Go now to Zarephath, which belongs to Sidon, and live there; for I have commanded a widow there to feed you." So he set out and went to Zarephath. When he came to the gate of the town, a widow was there gathering sticks; he called to her and said, "Bring me a little water in a vessel, so that I may drink." As she was going to bring it, he called to her and said, "Bring me a morsel of bread in your hand." But she said, "As the LORD your God lives, I have nothing baked, only a handful of meal in a jar, and a little oil in a jug; I am now gathering a couple of sticks, so that I may go home and prepare it for myself and my son, that we may eat it, and die." Elijah said to her, "Do not be afraid; go and do as you have said; but first make me a little cake of it and bring it to me, and afterwards make something for yourself and your son. For thus says the LORD the God of Israel: The jar of meal will not be emptied and the jug of oil will not fail until the day that the LORD sends rain on the earth." She went and did as Elijah said, so that she as well as he and her household ate for many days. The jar of meal was not emptied, neither did the jug of oil fail, according to the word of the LORD that he spoke by Elijah. After this the son of the woman, the mistress of the house, became ill; his illness was so severe that there was no breath left in him. She then said to Elijah, "What have you against me, O man of God? You have come to me to bring my sin to remembrance, and to cause the death of my son!" But he said to her, "Give me your son." He took him from her bosom, carried him up into the upper chamber where he was lodging, and laid him on his own bed. He cried out to the LORD, "O LORD my God, have you brought calamity even upon the widow with whom I am staying, by killing her son?" Then he stretched himself upon the child three times, and cried out to the LORD, "O LORD my God, let this child's life come into him again." The LORD listened to the voice of Elijah; the life of the child came into him again, and he revived. Elijah took the child, brought him down from the upper chamber into the house, and gave him to his mother; then Elijah said, "See, your son is alive." So the woman said to Elijah, "Now I know that you are a man of God, and that the word of the LORD in your mouth is truth." (1 Kings 17:8-24)

Have you noticed that it is God who initiates the change in our lives. It is God who sets in motion that which we need. It is God who acts first. Sometimes we think that we are the one seeking after God, but then later, we discover it was always God seeking to get our attention.

We see in the passage above how God initiates the action in the lives of the prophet Elijah and the widow of Sidon. God directs Elijah to a widow in Zarephath. God commands the widow to feed him. God makes it so that the jar of meal is not emptied and the jug of oil does not fail. God heals the widow's son.

God is constantly acting in their lives for their well-being. In the same way, God is acting in our lives. God is continually initiating a movement toward the building up of our lives. God acts and we respond. God acted in Elijah's life and he responded. God acted in the widow's life and she responded. It is not, we act and God responds. Even when we pray, it is because God has already moved on our hearts.

In fact, if we turn this around and start operating as if it is a matter of us acting and God responding, we generally get into trouble. We start acting as if by doing certain things we can leverage God to do for us in return. We think, "If I go to church and tithe, perhaps even go to Bible Study, maybe God will respond and give me what I think I need. If I sacrifice or fast, maybe God will give me what I want." But it is not like that with God. If I want my dog to do something, I can put a dogie cookie in front of her nose. I cannot do that with God.

God acts, and we respond. This is important for us to recognize because faith in God begins at the point where faith in our action ends. Faith in God begins when we turn from trusting in our own resources and circumstances and start believing in God.

God always initiates the action. In the beginning God created the heavens and the earth. And God so loved the world that *he* gave his only son. God is the good shepherd who leaves the ninety-nine and goes in search of the one lost sheep. We only come to God because he has been searching for us. We love him because he first loved us. It is God who takes the initiative in his relationship with us.

God, our good shepherd, chases us down. He comes knocking on the door of our heart and keeps coming because he loves us. He sees us caught in a thorn bush or in a ditch, hungry and thirsty. He comes to free us and lead us out into green pastures beside still waters where he restores our soul.

God came to Elijah in the midst of a drought and to a woman and her son on the verge of starvation, and God directed, provided and healed. God acted for their sake. They responded by trusting and obeying. God directed Elijah to a widow in Sidon, and Elijah responded by obeying God and going to Sidon. God commanded the widow to feed him, and the widow fed him. And God brought blessing, provisions and healing into their lives. It sounds so simple. God acts, we respond, and we are blessed.

If God provides for us, gives us what we need, brings healing and restores life, why do we not always respond in faith and obedience? Here is what is going on: When God acts in our lives, there are other things acting on our lives. We never respond to God in a vacuum. It is not like there is nothing else going on that can trip us up. When Elijah had to decide to obey God, he was being directed to a widow who had no visible means of support. She and her son were on the verge of starvation, and God sent Elijah to her, telling him that she would feed him! If Elijah was going to respond to God's action he was going to have to go to a woman with no resources to feed him, and in that situation, trust God!

If Elijah is going to obey God, he had better not spend time looking at the situation. Otherwise, he will be tempted to say, "God you must have it wrong. There is nothing here for me." This is true for the woman as well. She has nothing extra to give. She says, "As the LORD your God lives, I have nothing baked, only a handful of meal in a jar, and a little oil in a jug; I am now gathering a couple of sticks, so that I may go home and prepare it for myself and my son, that we may eat it, and die."

She had to believe in the face of the impossible, as far as the circumstances were concerned. Elijah said to her, "Do not be afraid; go and do as you have said; but first make me a little cake of it and bring it to me, and afterwards make something for yourself and your son. For thus says the LORD the God of Israel: The jar of meal will not be emptied and the jug of oil will not fail until the day that the LORD sends rain on the earth." The widow responded: "She went and did as Elijah said, so that she as well as he and her household ate for many days."

When her son became ill so that there was no breath in him, she had to believe again in the face of the impossible and bring her son to the prophet, Elijah. The prophet had to depend on God for the healing of her son. It was because of the response of faith that "the LORD listened to the voice of Elijah; the life of the child came into him again, and he revived."

Faith in God begins at the point where faith in our actions end. Faith in God begins when faith in our resources ends. When we no longer believe that the circumstances or the resources we have are going to save us or fix things, it is at that point that trust in God can truly begin.

We are so accustomed to judging and deciding on the basis of our circumstances. We check our resources, and then decide what is manageable. We check to see how much money we have. We make decisions about our abilities. When we come to the end of our resources, however, and God is directing us in a way that moves us beyond those resources, we are being called to trust in God. We are being called into a journey of faith where we have to learn over and over again to check for God's will first and then trust that God will provide.

We have discovered this reality in the life of the congregation I serve. When we started focusing on the ministry that God was raising up instead of our little resources, we found that we were no longer worrying over our resources. And God was providing.

God will take us to places where we have no resources other than what God provides. When my three year old brother died of leukemia–I was thirteen at the time—I found myself in the midst of things I could not understand

and could do nothing about. In my helplessness, I came to believe in the resurrection from the dead and believe the words on my brother's grave stone, "At home in the arms of Jesus." When I was a young man and realized that God wanted to reign over everything in my life, I found myself called to do something I could not do and that is to give up all right to myself. I prayed for months, "Lord make me willing to be willing." He did what I was unable to do for myself. He enabled me to let go and let him be God.

When I found myself trying to think my way to God, I finally had to come to the end of my thinking and despair of it, and put my faith in him. I discovered that I could not think my way to God. But I could trust God and begin to think from the starting point of faith. Each time I have been brought face to face with my own weakness and vulnerability, I have found myself left with no other real alternative but to trust. Faith in God begins at the point where faith in our resources and actions end.

Some have come to the place where they realized that their addiction to a chemical substance was out of their control. For a period of time, they tried to convince themselves that they could still overcome it—that they had the resources in themselves or that maybe a change in circumstances would make the difference—but then they came to a place where they said, "My life has become unmanageable and I cannot save myself. I need a higher power."

Some have been carried along by desires or lusts that have captivated and captured them for years. Their lives have become unhealthy and their relationships strained or broken by these obsessions. Others have been bound by internal hurts and grudges that have been carried for many years. They may have made many attempts to get free to no avail. They came to the "end of their rope" and reached out to one who sets the captive free. Still others have considered the brokenness of their own bodies and realized the situation had become unmanageable and the damage had been done, but that did not prevent them from going to God for their healing. God could do for them what they and the doctors could not do for themselves.

Faith in God begins at the point where faith in circumstances ends. Sometimes God allows us to live with our circumstances and feel the limits of them until, like a child who tries to lift something too big reaches out to her mother, we reach out for God's help. God will direct us in ways that bring faith in circumstances to an end, because faith in God begins where faith in our circumstances end.

I notice Elijah had already learned to believe and obey quickly. With the widow, more experience was needed. She had to learn to hear God's direction consistently over time in order to more quickly respond—as it is with us.

As we learn to hear the voice of God, we may find ourselves being called to actions that we could not imagine for ourselves. We end up moving out of our comfort zones and taking risks because God has called us into the future he has for us. When we stop listening to God we generally end up back in a comfort zone, a place where we feel we do not need to depend on God because we are again relying on our familiar situation and resources.

My brother, my sister, would you like to grow in faith and in the power of God? Simply do what God calls you to do! Go out and proclaim the reign of God and heal and deliver in the name of Jesus. That is what Jesus sends his followers to do. Go and make disciples. Proclaim God's kingdom. Bring healing and liberation in the power of the Spirit.

But maybe you are saying, "I am the one who needs healing and deliverance. I do not know about this thing of going to others. I am trying to get to God for myself." My sister, my brother, God is trying to get to you. God comes to you with deliverance, but his rescue demands everything. It demands your life. Even now he is calling forth faith from you. Faith is a little like sitting down on a chair. You have not sat down until you have rested all your weight on the chair, trusting it to hold you. Faith in God means resting our lives in him, trusting our whole self to him. God is present right now to help you with this. Only reach out to him. Seek and you will find.

5 Where The Lord Is There Is Freedom

Since, then, we have such a hope, we act with great boldness, not like Moses, who put a veil over his face to keep the people of Israel from gazing at the end of the glory that was being set aside. But their minds were hardened. Indeed, to this very day, when they hear the reading of the old covenant, that same veil is still there, since only in Christ is it set aside. Indeed, to this very day whenever Moses is read, a veil lies over their minds; but when one turns to the Lord, the veil is removed. Now the Lord is the Spirit, and where the Spirit of the Lord is, there is freedom. And all of us, with unveiled faces, seeing the glory of the Lord as though reflected in a mirror, are being transformed into the same image from one degree of glory to another; for this comes from the Lord, the Spirit. Therefore, since it is by God's mercy that we are engaged in this ministry, we do not lose heart. We have renounced the shameful things that one hides; we refuse to practice cunning or to falsify God's word; but by the open statement of the truth we commend ourselves to the conscience of everyone in the sight of God. (2 Corinthians 3:12-14:2)

Where the Spirit of the Lord is, there is freedom! There is freedom to take down my masks, to be honest about

myself, and to admit that my life has become unmanageable and I cannot free myself. There is freedom to confess
my sins, to receive forgiveness and to forgive. There is
freedom to accept and love myself and love my neighbor,
speaking the truth in love. There is freedom to love and
trust God above all things, to hope and to embrace the
future as coming from God, to be in love with God. There
is freedom to do God's will, to obey God and respond
whole-heartedly to his word.

However, where the Spirit of the Lord is absent, there is
bondage. There is bondage to the masks I wear and the
walls I put up. There is bondage to lies, mistrust, anxiety, guilt and low self-esteem. There is bondage to envy,
jealousy, bitterness, grudges and unforgiveness. There
is bondage to discord toward my neighbor and selfish
ambition and dishonesty about myself. There is bondage
to a heart closed to the truth, fixated on self and past hurts,
and willful and disobedient toward God.

Where the Spirit of the Lord is, there is freedom. Where
the Spirit of the Lord is not, there is bondage.

There is a sense in which the Spirit of God is everywhere
and available to all: "Where can I go from your spirit?
Or where can I flee from your presence? If I ascend to
heaven, you are there; if I make my bed in Sheol, you
are there. If I take the wings of the morning and settle at
the farthest limits of the sea, even there your hand shall
lead me, and your right hand shall hold me fast" (Psalm
139:7-10). God's Spirit is everywhere! There is no where
we can go where God is not already.

And yet, the Spirit can be present and I not be in the
Spirit. I can be away from the Spirit of God: "Do not cast
me away from your presence, and do not take your holy
spirit from me" (Psalm 51:11). God's Spirit is everywhere,
and yet there is a sense in which we can be out of God's
presence and away from his Spirit.

Sometimes we say, "I am in a bad place in my life right now," or "I do not know where I am." We are not talking about physical location, but a state of being. Where the Spirit of the Lord is, there is freedom. The question is: Am I in the Spirit? Am I where the Spirit of the Lord is? Am I in the Spirit, or am I into something else?

If our desires rule over us and dictate how we live, then we are caught up in our desires and lusts, and there is bondage. But if the Holy Spirit rules in our hearts and enables us to say no to our lusts, there is freedom. We are in a bad place when we are being ruled by our desires and lusts. We are in a good place when we are living in and ruled by the Spirit. Where the Spirit of the Lord is, there is freedom.

When we are being ruled by our desires and lusts, there is a veil over our minds. We cannot understand the things of the Spirit, and our minds are hardened. We are caught up in the power of evil and ways the world operates. We do not know anything else. But Paul gives us good news: "When one turns to the Lord, the veil is removed." The veil over our minds that prevented us from knowing God's will and perceiving the things of the Spirit is removed. We are given eyes to see and ears to hear. God enlightens the eyes of our hearts. The word of the Lord is, "Repent! Turn around!" The Spirit has a place in hearts that have turned to the Lord and come to trust the Lord.

Left to ourselves, without the Spirit of God in our lives, we do not discern spiritual things. We do not acknowledge the Spirit's power. We are still trying to do it all in our own power. We are thinking it is up to us. There is a veil over our eyes. We desire; we want; we strive; we try harder; we make resolutions. We tell ourselves we are going to do better.

We are like someone who is trying to drive somewhere without gas in her car. The car is well made. It is in great mechanical condition. It has a beautiful engine. But without gas it goes no where. Of course, someone who is trying to drive a car without gas is confused and does not understand about cars. Someone who is always trying harder to do better without the Spirit does not understand the power of the Spirit. Without the Holy Spirit, we are confused and do not understand, and we are pushing and prodding and going no where. We are bound, and we are stuck. We keep doing the same sins over and over again and fall back into the same despair and depression. What we need is for the veil to come off our fixated minds so that we truly see, so that the eyes of our hearts are enlightened, and we comprehend the greatness of God's grace and power.

Elsewhere in the second letter to the Corinthian church, Paul writes of "strongholds." "The weapons of our warfare are not merely human, but they have divine power to destroy strongholds" (2 Corinthians 10:4). The divine power is the Holy Spirit. But what are the strongholds? They are "arguments and every proud obstacle raised up against the knowledge of God," and they are thoughts which Paul says we are to "take captive to obey Christ."

The strongholds are in our minds, hardened with veils over them. The strongholds are thoughts that must be taken captive to obey Christ because they take us away from God. They come against the knowledge of God to prevent us from becoming the people God created us to become.

We all have strongholds! If we know Christ today, we are battling strongholds. Some of us have never really been able to be consistent. That is because there is a stronghold. Some of us live by procrastination. That is a stronghold. Some of us are fault-finders. Some keep falling back into the same sin over and over again. Others are hesitant and fearful or live with despair. Others have been indifferent toward the things of God. They are self-satisfied. These are strongholds. These are strongholds of the mind. But what we must recognize is this: It takes divine power to destroy strongholds.

God has power to destroy that stronghold in your life. You have not been able to break it off you. God can do what you have been unable to do! He can remove that stronghold and that veil from your mind. Jesus tells us that the Spirit of truth comes to convince us that we are wrong about some things. We have strongholds in our minds that keep telling us lies about sin and righteousness and where the victory is to be found.

Now, a lie loses its power as soon as we see that it is a lie. When something we have believed is recognized as a lie, its stranglehold is immediately loosened. When, by the Holy Spirit at work in us, we acknowledge that the recurring thought, "I can't" is a lie, it ceases to have the same power over us. "I can't change." "I can't overcome this sin or this addiction." "I can't follow Jesus every day." "I can't give up everything to follow him." The "I can't" is a lie. When the veil is removed and we see that "we can do all things through him who strengthens us" and "we are more than conquerors through him who loved us," then the lie crumbles, and the stronghold is being destroyed.

If there is something in your life today that you now know is a lie, you already have power to begin to dismiss it. The Spirit of truth who reveals to you the lie and the stronghold gives you power to take it down. That is why *faith* is so important in the Bible. Will you believe God today? Will you take him at his word? Will you believe that "in Christ is [the veil] set aside." In Christ, there is new life for us. In Christ, there is divine power for destroying strongholds. In him, the veil is removed. And when the strongholds come down, there is freedom. It is no longer only talked about, but lived. Where the Spirit of the Lord is, there is freedom.

Has God been showing you strongholds in your life? If so, say, "Thank you Lord for giving me eyes to see!" Are you starting to see that these strongholds are thoughts in your mind and lies? Will you, with the help of the Holy Spirit, call them lies? If you are able to see that they are lies, then say again, "Thank you Lord for giving me eyes to see!" Are you turning to the Lord, the Spirit, for help, for divine power for victory? Are you receiving it by faith? Then say to the Lord, "Thank you, Lord, for removing the veil! Thank you for new life."

We are on a journey. "All of us, with unveiled faces, seeing the glory of the Lord as though reflected in a mirror, are being transformed into the same image from one degree of glory to another; for this comes from the Lord, the Spirit." With unveiled faces we are seeing that it is not about us. It is not about what we can do to get our lives back together. It is about the Lord, the Spirit. With the veils removed, we are seeing the glory of the Lord. We are seeing his victory. We are trusting in his power. In Christ, we are learning to take every thought captive. Through Christ who strengthens us, we are not letting lies dictate our lives. We are walking by faith, not by sight, and by the Spirit, not by the flesh, so that we are being transformed from one degree of glory to another. We are being transformed by God into the image of God. We are beginning to enjoy the freedom of the children of God who are led by the Holy Spirit. Where the Spirit of the Lord is, there is freedom!

God's Deliverance

A Meditation On Psalm 107

6 God Delivers People Living On Empty

O give thanks to the Lord, for he is good;
    for his steadfast love endures forever.
Let the redeemed of the Lord say so,
    those he redeemed from trouble
and gathered in from the lands,
    from the east and from the west,
    from the north and from the south.

Some wandered in desert wastes,
    finding no way to an inhabited town;
hungry and thirsty,
    their soul fainted within them.
Then they cried to the Lord in their trouble,
    and he delivered them from their distress;
he led them by a straight way,
    until they reached an inhabited town.
Let them thank the Lord for his steadfast love,
    for his wonderful works to humankind.
For he satisfies the thirsty,
    and the hungry he fills with good things.
        (Psalm 107:1-9)

After seventy years in captivity, the Lord made a way for the people of Israel to return to Jerusalem and Judea. They came from exile in Babylon and from foreign lands where many had fled. The Lord redeemed them from trouble and gathered them "in from the lands, from the east and from the west, from the north and from the south." They came back home where they began to rebuild Jerusalem and the temple and their lives.

Psalm 107 is a psalm that gives thanks to God for redeeming his people from their trouble. It gives thanks for release from bondage, so that they could rebuild their lives. It describes various kinds of deliverance. In this chapter, we focus on deliverance for those who wandered in desert wastes. God delivers people living on empty!

"Some wandered in desert wastes, finding no way to an inhabited town; hungry and thirsty, their soul fainted within them. Then they cried to the Lord in their trouble, and he delivered them from their distress." Some of those returning from captivity in Babylon got lost. They were in a waste place. They were without sustenance, and they languished.

We can get into waste places where there is no sustenance, where we are living on empty and feeling faint. We do not always know how we got there, but we know that is where we are. We feel like we have nothing to keep us going. We are not even sure where we should be going. We have lost our way. We are into activities that only deplete us. They give us nothing. We start asking questions like, "Who am I? Why am I here? Where am I going?" We are lost and empty.

Sometimes we talk about burnout. We have been active in various projects, trying to get aspects of our lives together. Maybe we have been serving and trying to help others, but we are feeling depleted and running on empty. We are losing our sense of direction, and we are unsure about why we are doing what we are doing. We question our purpose or calling. We question what we are about. We ask, "What am I doing here?" We feel that we have nothing more to give. We are ready to give up without knowing what we will do next.

Sometimes we have drifted away from God and from others that God has placed in our lives. We have drifted away from God's word which would have sustained us in our weariness. We may even have spiraled downward into depression or despair. And we do not know how to get out of it. We do not feel that we can go on.

Are you living on empty today? God delivers people living on empty! "Then they cried to the Lord in their trouble, and he delivered them from their distress." The major reason that we stay lost and running on empty is that we do not cry to the Lord in our trouble. We either are still trying to fill the emptiness with that which cannot sustain us, or we have despaired of God.

Only God can fill the emptiness, and yet we will try to fill it with various activities, work, parties, television, the internet and various kinds of relationships and, if we have some affluence, ever more possessions. But the emptiness will not be filled, and these things will not sustain us. We may try to cover the emptiness with alcohol or drugs or sex or various forms of escape, but as soon as the drug wears off or the activity is through, we will still be faced with the reality of our emptiness and loneliness and feelings of being lost.

It is time to cry out to the Lord in our trouble. "*Then* they cried to the Lord." Have you gotten to the *then* yet? You tried to find meaning in yet another relationship or activity or plan, but now you are through trying. *Then* you cried to the Lord. Or, you tried to get out off your depression by pursuing your desires and appetites, but things only got worse. You found yourself at the end of your resources. You are now exhausted. *Then* you cried to the Lord.

"Then they cried to the Lord, and he delivered them from their distress." God delivers people living on empty! God brings us back to what we truly need. We need him! Jesus said, "Blessed are those who hunger and thirst for righteousness, for they will be filled." The Lord is our righteousness.

We can spend so much time hungering and thirsting after that which will not fill us. Why is that? It is as if the thing that always left us unfulfilled in the past is going to do something different this time. It is time to stop believing the lie! Only the living God can fill the emptiness and loneliness. God alone delivers us. Do you want God to deliver you from that waste place you are in? If your answer to that question is yes, then here is the thing for you to do: Admit you are in trouble. Acknowledge before God that you cannot find your way out of your waste place, and cry out to the Lord. Those that cried out to the Lord in their trouble, the Scripture says, "He delivered them from their distress."

From our side, we are to cry out to the Lord. From God's side, this is what he does: (1) God leads us by a straight way. ("He led them by a straight way.") (2) God leads us into community. ("Until they reached an inhabited town.") (3) God fills us with good things. ("For he satisfies the thirsty, and the hungry he fills with good things.")

God leads us by a straight way.

Comfort, O comfort my people, says your God.
Speak tenderly to Jerusalem,
    and cry to her
that she has served her term,
    that her penalty is paid,
that she has received from the Lord's hand
    double for all her sins.

A voice cries out:
"In the wilderness prepare the way of the Lord,
    make straight in the desert a highway for our
      God.
Every valley shall be lifted up,
    and every mountain and hill be made low;
the uneven ground shall become level,
    and the rough places a plain." (Isaiah 40:1-4)

God leads by a straight way. No more twists and turns. No more uneven ground. It is a straight way back to Zion, back to the healing community of God's people. When we get off God's way it is on crooked paths, and convoluted and twisted side-tracks. There is nothing straight about the roads that evil takes us down. In fact, we make excuses for the roads we take. We rationalize. We can't be straightforward about what we are doing and where we are going. We tell ourselves, "It will be okay just this one time" or "No one is going to know" or "It is not that bad" or "Everyone is doing it" or "It is not going to hurt anyone" or "I really don't need to pray about this thing." (Of course, what we really mean is that we do not *want* to pray about this thing!)

We go this way, and then we go that way. The "father of liars," keeps feeding us more lies to block us from the truth. We are supplied with lie upon lie until we are in some waste place, wondering how we got there.

But God leads us by a straight way, the only way out of the waste place toward home! The word of truth leads us home. Jesus says, "Those who do what is true come to the light." Lies, excuses, rationalizations, self-justifications, the crooked way, only lead to desert waste places and more darkness and emptiness.

Thanks be to God that he comes to us in our waste places and speaks truth there. In the story of our alienation from God in the book of Genesis, God came to Adam after he had fallen to temptation. Adam was still in the Garden of Eden, but it had become a desert waste to him. God came to him where he was. He called to him saying, "Where are you?" The man said, "I heard the sound of you in the garden, and I was afraid, because I was naked; and I hid myself." In other words, I went down a crooked road. I did what the lie tempted me to do. ("You will not die; for God knows that when you eat of it your eyes will be opened, and you will be like God, knowing good and evil.") Now I am hiding. I am in a waste place. I feel exposed. The Lord said, "Who told you that you were naked? Have you eaten from the tree of which I commanded you not to eat?"

The Lord comes to us in our waste places where we are hiding and alone. He speaks truth into that place we have gotten ourselves. And we have to admit we are in trouble and need God. And God comes to lead us out of that place of emptiness. God leads us by a straight way. He speaks truth to us, about us. He brings us into the truth. He sends Jesus who says, "If you continue in my word, you are truly my disciples; and you will know the truth, and the truth will make you free" (John 8:32).

God leads us into community.

God led them "by a straight way, until they reached an inhabited town."

God knows that we cannot make it on our own. We are not islands unto ourselves. He created us for relationship. He made us to live in community. Our healing and new life is found in the community of faith. That is why Jesus gathered a community of followers around him. That is why we gather together in communities of faith that acknowledge the presence of God. The Spirit of God gathers us into true community that is held together by Jesus Christ, God's Word. When I see people gather together into the sanctuary of our church, I see the gathering work of God's Spirit. When I see people responding to God's word, praying for each other, ministering to each other with their individual gifts, I see God's Spirit at work. It is in the fellowship of God's people that there is sustenance for life's journey.

God leads us into community where we discover God's love and receive the ministry of God's Word and learn to pray for one another. We are, each of us, like living stones being built into a spiritual house. We are given gifts of the Spirit and different ways of serving so that the community of God's people might be built up. It is critical for rebuilding our lives. God made us that way. God brings us into community.

God fills us with good things.

"*God* satisfies the thirsty, and the hungry he fills with good things." The emphasis is on "God." Our problem is that we have acted like it was up to us to fill ourselves with good things. And we have been like children who want to eat sweets all the time. Thankfully, parents will generally step in with a balanced diet for their children. Left to ourselves, we will try to fill up on that which does not satisfy and ignore what truly gives life, but God, our parent, gives us what we truly need.

God brings us into his family. Among our brothers and sisters, we receive God's good news and the Holy Spirit and new life. We receive healing and deliverance. Things that have been wrong are being made right. We are being filled with good things. The void in our lives is being filled by God. The hunger of our souls is being satisfied. And God is doing it! And the other concerns—the things we get anxious about, the lesser things, food, clothing and shelter—God takes care of these as well. But we are reminded to keep our priorities straight. "Strive first for God's kingdom and God's righteousness and all these other things will be yours as well" (Matthew 6:33). It is God who fills the emptiness. It is God who delivers us from the waste places. The lesser things cannot do it.

God wants to fill the empty place in our hearts with his presence and our relationships with his love and truth. God desires for us to be real with him and with one another and to speak the truth in love and welcome one another in love. God fills us with good things!

Are you in a desert waste today? Have you been running on empty? Are you nearing burnout? Have you gotten your priorities mixed up? Have you been majoring in minors and minoring in majors? Have you traded in your first love for lesser things? Have you gone down false paths? Have you gotten sidetracked? Cry out to the Lord in your trouble. Turn from the things you have been grasping at and running after, and cry out to the Lord. He will deliver you from your distress. Right now, reach out to the Lord and cry out, "Save me!" God is present to save. Let him. And then thank him: "O give thanks to the Lord, for he is good; for his steadfast love endures forever. Let the redeemed of the Lord say so, those he redeemed from trouble."

7 God Delivers People In Bondage

Some sat in darkness and in gloom,
    prisoners in misery and in irons,
for they had rebelled against the words of God,
    and spurned the counsel of the Most High.
Their hearts were bowed down with hard labor;
    they fell down, with no one to help.
Then they cried to the Lord in their trouble,
    and he saved them from their distress;
he brought them out of darkness and gloom,
    and broke their bonds asunder.
Let them thank the Lord for his steadfast love,
    for his wonderful works to humankind.
For he shatters the doors of bronze,
    and cuts in two the bars of iron.
        (Psalm 107:10-16)

"Some sat in darkness and in gloom, prisoners in misery and in irons." We are told why they were prisoners in misery and gloom: "They had rebelled against the words of God, and spurned the counsel of the Most High." God's judgment against them had been announced by Jeremiah and Ezekiel and other prophets. Jeremiah proclaimed it: "The word of the Lord came to me a second time, saying, 'What do you see?' And I said, 'I see a boiling pot, tilted away from the north.' Then the Lord said to me: 'Out of the north disaster shall break out on all the inhabitants of the

51

land. For now I am calling all the tribes of the kingdoms of the north, says the Lord; and they shall come and all of them shall set their thrones at the entrance of the gates of Jerusalem, against all its surrounding walls and against all the cities of Judah. And I will utter my judgments against them, for all their wickedness in forsaking me; they have made offerings to other gods, and worshiped the works of their own hands'" (Jeremiah 1:13-16).

The Babylonians came from the north and swept down on Judea and Jerusalem and laid waste the city and took the people captive, bringing them to Babylon where they remained in bondage for seventy years, where they "sat in darkness and in gloom, prisoners in misery and in irons. Their hearts were bowed down with hard labor; they fell down, with no one to help."

When we are in captivity, whether of someone else's making or our own, we are bowed down and without help, left to ourselves. With chains holding us fast and unable to break the bonds, someone is going to have to come and set us free. "Then they cried to the Lord in their trouble, and he saved them from their distress; he brought them out of darkness and gloom, and broke their bonds asunder." This word is about being set free from that which binds us. It is about what must happen for us to be made free.

We know that bondage takes many forms, and one form can give way to another. Bondage can be physical, but it can also be mental or spiritual. In Frederick Douglass' *My Bondage and My Freedom,* Douglass gives a defense for those few slaves that having run for freedom and arriving in a free state, nevertheless, end up returning to the slave holder:

A freeman cannot understand why the slave master's shadow is bigger, to the slave, than the might and majesty of a free state; but when he reflects that the slave knows more about the slavery of his master than he does of the might and majesty of the free state, he has the explanation. The slave has been all his life learning the power of his master— being trained to dread his approach—and only a few hours learning the power of the state. The master is to him a stern and flinty reality, but the state is little more than a dream.

We battle with bondage in heart and mind. Long after the chemical aspects of drug addiction have worn off, there often remain the emotional and mental aspects of addiction. The obsessions that we have had for years do not generally disappear in a night. The habits formed over time do not lose their hold the moment we decide to break the habit. The appetites and lusts and greed that we have entertained and nourished don't lose their power in the moment that we say, "I really don't want to live this way anymore."

We have to face down our fear many times in the strength of the Lord before it is overcome. We have to grow in believing in God's power in order to be loosed from our belief in the power that for years has had us bound. In God's presence, we experience freedom from that which has long held us in bondage. We must *grow* in him and the freedom we have in him.

We know that children of addicts carry with them into adulthood coping mechanisms which also enslave and interfere in relationships. But not only children of addicts. Children dealing with any kind of family dysfunction— abuse, emotional manipulation, sickness or death in the family—do what they can to survive. Children, like adults, will do what makes sense to make their way through the difficulties. Like us, they will try to save themselves out of a bad situation. One child will become the responsible child, trying to be the parent when the parent is absent by virtue of the effects of a drug. Another will be the adjuster, attempting to "go with the flow." Another, the placater, will try to please everybody. Still another will "act out" in a plea for help. They survive childhood, but they carry mental strongholds into adulthood. They have learned not to talk about things, not to trust others and not to feel. And each one has taken on a role with a downside.

The placater has learned to survive by caring for the other broken members of the family, showing empathy and sensitivity and being a good listener. The placater gives and gives with a nice smile. The downside is that she is unable to receive, unable to focus on her self and identify her needs. She suffers with guilt because she can never do enough to make things right for others. She tolerates all kinds of inappropriate behavior.

Claudia Black in her book, *It Will Never Happen To Me*, shares her experience with a forty-four year old woman who had played out the placater role. She grew up with two alcoholic parents—and had learned to placate. As an adult she ended up in marriages to three practicing alcoholics. (She was good at taking care of alcoholics! It was familiar, comfortable territory.) Her third husband finally ended up hospitalized for his alcoholism, and she was going to have three weeks away from him and from any responsibility for him. Dr. Black sat down with her and asked her the question: "Elaine, while your husband is in the hospital for the next three weeks, what can you do for you so you'll feel better." Dr. Black had to ask this question several times while Elaine turned away from her, grimacing and then starting to shake. "Elaine, you don't have to take care of your husband anymore. We are going to do that. So, what are you going to do for you?" Elaine, finally with tears running down her face said in a whisper, "I don't know. I don't know."

That is bondage, when we do not know how to care for ourselves and do not know how to ask for or receive help. Jesus tells us to love our neighbor as ourselves, which means we have to be able to love ourselves. The good news is that God comes to us where we are bound. God cares about these mental bondages that keep us from the life he has for us, that get us stuck, that keep us from growing up into the new life of freedom that he has for us.

"Then they cried to the Lord in their trouble." For our part, we must want our freedom enough to cry out to the Lord for his help. Jesus says, "Seek and you will find; knock and the door will be open; ask and it will be given you."

Are you tired of the bondage? Are you tired of being held down and held back? Are you tired of the mental stronghold that has you going back to the same old thing that has been hurting you and stunting your growth in the Lord? Are you tired and weary? Do you want to be free? "Seek and you will find." Cry out to the Lord in your trouble.

Frederick Douglass shares about a man, an elder who was also enslaved, who became a mentor to him:

> The advice and the suggestions of Uncle Lawson, were not without their influence upon my character and destiny. He threw my thoughts into a channel from which they have never entirely diverged. He fanned my already intense love of knowledge into a flame, by assuring me that I was to be a useful man in the world. When I would say to him, "How can these things be and what can I do?" his simple reply was, "Trust in the Lord." When I told him that "I was a slave, and a slave FOR LIFE," he said, "the Lord can make you free, my dear. All things are possible with him, only have faith in God." "Ask,

and it shall be given." "If you want liberty," said the good old man, "ask the Lord for it, in faith, AND HE WILL GIVE IT TO YOU."

"Then they cried to the Lord in their trouble, and he saved them from their distress; he brought them out of darkness and gloom, and broke their bonds asunder." Two things that the Lord did: (1) He brought them out of darkness and gloom; and (2) He broke their bonds asunder. The first has to do with knowledge and the second, with power.

God brings us out of darkness and gloom.

God opens the eyes of our hearts. He enables us to see things about ourselves and about him and how he works. For a brief period of time Frederick Douglass—still a boy and very young—had a mistress who started to help him with reading until her husband found out and forbade her to teach him anymore. Douglass received a revelation from this situation: "It was a new and special revelation, dispelling a painful mystery, against which my youthful understanding had struggled, and struggled in vain, to wit: the white man's power to perpetuate the enslavement of the black man." Douglass realized that the slave holder maintained his power by making sure the black man was not educated. "'Very well,' thought I; 'knowledge unfits a child to be a slave.' I instinctively assented to the proposition; and from that moment I understood the direct pathway from slavery to freedom." Douglass made it a point to get knowledge.

God brings us out of darkness and gloom. He brings us out of the fog that has settled upon our lives. He opens the eyes of our hearts. He gives us understanding. He helps us to see what is enslaving us and what is getting in the way and what is hurting us.

When Jesus speaks about the coming of the Spirit of truth and what the Spirit will do in our lives, he speaks of the Spirit bringing us knowledge: "When the Spirit of truth comes, he will guide you into all the truth; for he will not speak on his own, but will speak whatever he hears, and he will declare to you the things that are to come" (John 16:13). God brings us out of darkness and gloom. He brings us into the light, so that we see things we did not see before. He reveals to us ourselves and reveals his plans for us. This is why it is so important for us to listen to him.

God breaks our bonds asunder.

God does for us what we cannot do for ourselves. God breaks strongholds. Through Christ Jesus, every thought is to be made captive to obey God. In Christ, there is victory to be received by faith! Jesus says to us, "So if the Son makes you free, you will be free indeed." But before he says these words, he says: "If you continue in my word, you are truly my disciples; and you will know the truth, and the truth will make you free" (John 8:31-36).

God has broken our bonds asunder in Jesus Christ, but now we must walk in our freedom by faith. We must walk by the Spirit and live in the freedom that is ours in Christ Jesus. Believe it and receive it and walk in it. It is there for us. God is calling us to take steps of faith. "If you continue in my word...you will know the truth, and the truth will make you free." If you take the steps I am giving you to take, you will come to know truth about yourself, and that truth will make you free.

There are yokes that have been broken *in Christ* that we do not yet experience as broken, because we are going to have to believe it. We are going to have to step out in faith. We are going to have to start acting like they really are broken through Christ Jesus. There is a sense in which Frederick Douglass got set free long before he escaped and experienced the freedom of being in a free state. Something had happened inside him. A light had come in, a revelation and a faith and a passion that refused to be a slave any longer. He came to stand up for his freedom well before he escaped to freedom. He had come to see some things:

> The old doctrine that submission is the very best cure for outrage and wrong, does not hold good on the slave plantation. He is whipped oftenest, who is whipped easiest; and that slave who has the courage to stand up for himself against the overseer, although he may have many hard stripes at the first, becomes, in the end, a freeman, even though he sustain the formal relation of a slave. "You can shoot me but you can't whip me," said a slave to Rigby Hopkins; and the result was that he was neither whipped nor shot.

That which has had you bound and beaten, will you believe that you are free and stand up and face it in the name of Jesus Christ? Do it today. Do not be unbelieving, but believing. Our main struggle is with belief, and while we struggle with belief, we desperately need the body of Christ. We need believers around us. We need those who will encourage us, "Walk by faith, not by sight."

You see that which has had you bound. The tempter is saying, "It is too strong for you." Say, "Get behind me Satan in the name of Jesus. What is too strong for me is not too strong for my Lord, and he has already overcome it. I am more than a conqueror through him who loves me."

Trust in the Lord! Cry out to the Lord, and trust him in what he is doing. *Walking* by faith is so very important. We are involved in a walk. "If you continue in my word...the truth will make you free." Keep facing down those things that have you bound and do so day by day, moment by moment, and experience the power of God. And then thank the Lord: "Let them thank the Lord for his steadfast love, for his wonderful works to humankind. For he shatters the doors of bronze, and cuts in two the bars of iron."

8 God Delivers People Who Are Sick

> Some were sick through their sinful ways,
>> and because of their iniquities endured afflic-
>>> tion;
> they loathed any kind of food,
>> and they drew near to the gates of death.
> Then they cried to the Lord in their trouble,
>> and he saved them from their distress;
> he sent out his word and healed them,
>> and delivered them from destruction.
> Let them thank the Lord for his steadfast love,
>> for his wonderful works to humankind.
> And let them offer thanksgiving sacrifices,
>> and tell of his deeds with songs of joy.
>> (Psalm 107:17-22)

"Some were sick through their sinful ways." We can get sick through our sinful ways. It is not, of course, the only way we get sick. We can get sick simply from living in a world where there is disease. We can catch a virus. But here it says that "some were sick through their sinful ways." They didn't just catch something, but rather it is "because of their iniquities that they endured affliction."

We do know that our sinful ways can affect our bodies. Paul writes: "Shun fornication! Every sin that a person commits is outside the body; but the fornicator sins against the body itself. Or do you not know that your body is a temple of the Holy Spirit within you, which you have from God, and that you are not your own? For you were bought with a price; therefore glorify God in your body" (1 Corinthians 6:18-20). If we are not glorifying God in our body, then we open up our bodies to various forms of breakdown.

We can sin against the body itself, which is the temple of the Holy Spirit. We can put drugs into our bodies. We can sniff, swallow and insert substances that do direct harm to the body. We can eat things that are detrimental to our health. Our diets can harm the temple. We can sin in this area both by what we commit and what we omit, by what we do to our bodies and by the absence of care for our bodies. We can have a life-style that opens us up to sexually transmitted diseases and thereby sin against our bodies, and be sick through our sinful ways.

There are other more indirect ways that our sin affects the health of our bodies. "While I kept silence, my body wasted away through my groaning all day long. For day and night your hand was heavy upon me; my strength was dried up as by the heat of summer. Then I acknowledged my sin to you, and I did not hide my iniquity; I said, 'I will confess my transgressions to the Lord,' and you forgave the guilt of my sin" (Psalm 32:3-5). Sin and guilt affect our physical well-being. Anxiety and not trusting in God affect us. Guilt can lead us into depression and anxiety into stress related diseases. Sin robs us of joy and peace, and our emotional breakdown affects our bodies. Our immune systems can be affected so that we are unable to fend off diseases that we would otherwise have fended off. Some forms of behavior catch up with us over many years.

We can even get to a place where we "loath any kind of food, and draw near to the gates of death." It may be at that point we finally cry out to the Lord: "Then they cried to the Lord in their trouble, and he saved them from their distress." At such times we may ask questions for self-examination: Have we been sinning against the Holy Spirit's temple? Do we see that our guilt and unbelief have affected our emotional and physical well-being? Can we get specific about our sins? Are we ready to turn to the Lord and cry out in our trouble? He will hear our prayer and act.

God sends out his word and heals us.

"He sent out his word and healed them." By God's word, we are healed! "When [Jesus] entered Capernaum, a centurion came to him, appealing to him and saying, 'Lord, my servant is lying at home paralyzed, in terrible distress.' And he said to him, 'I will come and cure him.' The centurion answered, 'Lord, I am not worthy to have you come under my roof; but only speak the word, and my servant will be healed.' Jesus said, 'Go; let it be done for you according to your faith.' And the servant was healed in that hour" (Matthew 8:5-8,13). It is by God's word that all things are created. It is by God's word that we are healed. The centurion who understood authority knew by faith who has authority over disease. "Just speak the word, Jesus."

The God who created and redeemed us has healing for us. He wants us to go to him for our healing. He wants us to receive his word that we might be healed. By faith and obedience to his word we are healed.

The first word he speaks to us when we cry out to him may not be related to our physical healing. The paralyzed man whose friends brought him to Jesus was told his sins were forgiven before he was told to take up his bed and walk. God's first word to us may be, "Repent!" Turn from putting into your body that which is destroying it. Turn from that life-style which is unhealthy to soul and body.

God's first word may be, "Fear not, for I am with you." We have been sick with fear, and God's word of assurance relieves us. God's word may be, "There is therefore now no condemnation for those who are in Christ Jesus." We have been overwhelmed by guilt. We may be like the woman caught in adultery who hears the words of Jesus, "I do not condemn you. Go and sin no more." God sends out his word, and by his word, heals us.

What is God saying to you today? His word will heal and restore you—spiritually, emotionally and physically. Do not push away his word. Sometimes, as parents, we will complain that our children have selective hearing. Sometimes, as children of our heavenly Father, we have selective hearing. What is God saying to us today? He has a specific word for each of us. What he has to say to us is not always the first thing we want to hear, but it will lead to our healing if we trust him and obey his word.

If we are open to the word our Father is speaking, willing to hear him no matter what he has to say to us, we will recognize his voice. "Anyone who resolves to do the will of God will know whether the teaching is from God" (John 7:17). We do not have to go running around lost, limping between allegiances. God wants us to know his direction and his word for us. Therefore, let us be *willing* to do his will so that we might perceive it.

If we are truly open, we will find that God's word is like a scalpel. "The word of God is living and active, sharper than any two-edged sword, piercing until it divides soul from spirit, joints from marrow; it is able to judge the thoughts and intentions of the heart" (Hebrews 4:12). It cuts deep into us. It gets at places that we do not reach. God is like a physician who knows exactly what must come out. He calls it out. We have to confess it out, sometimes to one another.

"Welcome with meekness the implanted word that has the power to save your souls" (James 1:21). What is God saying to you right now? There is healing for you in what God is saying. There is new life in his direction, and in the truth. There is no healing in what you have been telling yourself when you have tried to deny what was going on with you. Will you believe what God is saying?

Sometimes our past catches up with us. Our past hurts, decisions and abuse make us sick. There are situations—and even forms of ministry—that we will avoid because they affect us emotionally and physically. They touch on that which from our past makes us sick. The good news is that there is healing for those past hurts. They do not have to continually get in the way of what God wants to do in and through us.

There is healing for you right now in what God is saying to you. Is he saying to you that you are more than a conqueror through Christ? Believe him today! Is he calling you to press forward in the face of fear? He is saying to you, "Do not be afraid, for I am with you to accomplish in and through you what I have already planned beforehand for you." The Lord is saying, "Trust me at my word, and obey me!" There is healing for you in God's word and call!

God delivers us from destruction.

"God delivered them from destruction." Left to ourselves, without God's word, we will destroy ourselves. We will end up in bondage to fear, and we will make ourselves sick with fear. Or, we will end up in bondage to our desires and appetites, and we will make ourselves sick from our lusts and dissipation and drunkenness and overindulging. Or, we will be in bondage to our hurts, and we will make ourselves sick with bitterness and unforgiveness and complaining. Or, we will be in bondage to guilt and fall into depression and isolate ourselves, cutting ourselves off from others. Or, we will be in bondage to pride, and in our arrogance tell ourselves that we are strong and will not fall to temptation. But as Paul says, "Pride goes before the fall," and we will fall into all the kinds of temptations that others have fallen into, and we will be brought low. Left to ourselves, we will destroy ourselves, our lives and our relationships.

God comes to us to deliver us from self-destruction. Will you let him do that today? Jesus says that there is a broad, easy road that leads to destruction and many are on it. Jesus tells us about this road as a warning because he does not want us to stay on it and be destroyed. He tells us that there is another road that leads to eternal life. That road is hard and narrow. It is the hard narrow road of God's word. Through Christ Jesus, we come to be on that road. Through Christ Jesus, who has come to live in us, we learn to walk by faith, not by sight, and by the Spirit, not by the flesh.

This is not a religious road. It is a relationship road. God did not call us to a form of religion where we could get comfortable with religious words, but he called us to a relationship in which we must now grow as we respond to the voice of God. God delivers us from destruction, by bringing us into a relationship with himself. Paul writes: "I want to know Christ and the power of his resurrection and the sharing of his sufferings by becoming like him in his death, if somehow I may attain the resurrection from the dead. Not that I have already obtained this or have already reached the goal; but I press on to make it my own, because Christ Jesus has made me his own" (Philippians 3:10-12). We have reason to press on in this relationship with Christ, to share in his victory and his suffering. In him, we experience the new life.

In Christ, we have our complete healing. By his stripes we are healed. Perhaps we feel that we have already made a complete mess of it. Perhaps we look at our self-destruction and wonder if we can still be healed. God has healing for us! It is not a matter of how well we have destroyed things, but how great God is at restoring.

> Then they cried to the Lord in their trouble, and he saved them from their distress; he sent out his word and healed them, and delivered them from destruction. Let them thank the Lord for his steadfast love, for his wonderful works to humankind. And let them offer thanksgiving sacrifices, and tell of his deeds with songs of joy.

Sometimes it is on our way to offer thanksgiving sacrifices that the healing comes. Jesus said to ten lepers, "'Go and show yourselves to the priests.' And as they went, they were made clean" (Luke 17:14). Sometimes it is a matter of turning our attention from the leprosy and our frantically trying to figure out how we are going to fix it, and start worshiping the Lord, bowing down before him with our disease, acknowledging his power and majesty and sovereignty.

> I am the God, that healeth thee
> I am the Lord your healer
> I sent My word and healed your disease
> I am the Lord, your healer (Song by Don Moen)

9 God Delivers People Overcome By Fear

Some went down to the sea in ships,
    doing business on the mighty waters;
they saw the deeds of the Lord,
    his wondrous works in the deep.
For he commanded and raised the stormy wind,
    which lifted up the waves of the sea.
They mounted up to heaven, they went down to
      the depths;
    their courage melted away in their calamity;
they reeled and staggered like drunkards,
    and were at their wits' end.
Then they cried to the Lord in their trouble,
    and he brought them out from their distress;
he made the storm be still,
    and the waves of the sea were hushed.
Then they were glad because they had quiet,
    and he brought them to their desired haven.
Let them thank the Lord for his steadfast love,
    for his wonderful works to humankind.
Let them extol him in the congregation of the
      people,
    and praise him in the assembly of the elders.
    (Psalm 107:23-32)

The nearest I came to panic was when I got caught in a rip tide in the Pacific Ocean on the California coast. I was in my late teens trying to swim back to shore and losing ground swimming against the current. I was steadily being pulled out to sea despite my best efforts, and I was becoming exhausted. Fear began to take hold. It clutched at me and started to gain a stranglehold. Panic was about to rob me of my remaining strength. I found myself fighting against fear, sensing that giving into it would mean that all would be lost. In the midst of the struggle, it came to me that I needed to swim diagonally to the shore. Little by little, I began to gain ground until I finally reached land.

Fear, dread, panic, terror. "Their courage melted. They reeled and staggered and were at their wits' end." In Psalm 107, those who went down to the sea were simply going to work. They were "doing business on the mighty waters." But they were unsettled by a "stormy wind, which lifted up the waves of the sea" and caused them to reel and stagger like drunkards. That which unsettles us, like waves of the sea tossing us around, demonstrates that we are not in control. In Psalm 107, it is the "deeds of the Lord, his wondrous works in the deep" that unsettle those going about their seafaring business. They were, in fact, unsettled by God's power. God "commanded and raised the stormy wind."

We, like them, are also afraid of God's power. We are afraid of not being in control, but God created us in such a way that we have to face much in life that is out of our control. We face situations, circumstances, people, unplanned disturbances, realities outside us and inside us that are out of our control. We are often unsettled by storms within that come in the form of past hurts. We have wounds inflicted in past relationships and experiences. We carry slights and grievances, abuse and trauma, that have added up over time. These hurts come back, at times, as storms that play havoc with our present circumstances. Some situations we avoid because of fears issuing from past hurts. Other situations we remain guarded and defensive about. Unresolved hurts and pain in our lives stir up inner storms when given the right conditions.

Some storms will bring us to our "wits' end." Are you at your wits' end? In what area of your life and in what circumstances do you tend to "lose it?" There is something we can do when we get to our wits' end. We can even do it before we get there: "Then they cried to the Lord in their trouble." Notice what God does when we cry to him: God "brought them out from their distress; he made the storm be still, and the waves of the sea were hushed. Then they were glad because they had quiet, and he brought them to their desired haven."

God brings us out from our distress.

Are you ready for God to bring you out of your distress? Or, are you going to try to manage on your own a little longer? Have you come to your wits' end? Is your wisdom at an end? Do you know you need God's wisdom today? Are you through trying to set things right according to your own understanding? Do you now know that God is going to have to bring you out of your distress?

Have you got to the "then" yet? "*Then* they cried to the Lord in their trouble, and he brought them out from their distress." The thing that most gets in the way of our experiencing God's deliverance is that we still think we can work it out on our own. God will let us try until things unravel to the point where we finally cry out to him. Sometimes, as parents, we will let our children try to do something we know is not going to work until, in frustration, they come to us and ask us to show them how to do it. God will let us get to a place of fear as we see things falling apart so that we might finally come to him and receive from him what he has had for us all along. "It was grace that taught my heart to fear and grace my fears relieved" (*Amazing Grace*).

Unhealed hurt in our lives will cause us all kinds of problems. Unhealed hurt from a past relationship will stop us from entering another relationship. Unhealed hurt that comes from sexual abuse, will cause problems with intimacy in marriage. Unhealed hurt that comes from emotional abuse and growing up in the midst of negativity will stop us from attempting new ventures. On the verge of a new undertaking, fear will well up in us. We will say, "I can't."

Fear can stop us, fear of failure, fear of success, fear of loss, fear of rejection, fear of commitment. Unhealed hurts and the resulting fears can keep us from what God has for us. Hurt and fear are stopping many of our young people who do not finish high school or other endeavors and end up jobless with more hurt and fear.

Some of us will try to get our act together, as we say. We will assure ourselves that we are survivors. And yet, we get stopped by storms we carry within us as well as the ones we face in the world. We get stopped from God's purpose for us. But we are not left without help. God has given us something to do. From that place of distress, we are to cry to the Lord, and he will hear our cry, and he will deliver us from our distress. He "makes the storm be still, and hushes the waves of the sea."

God wants to get at those storms in our lives. He wants us to give up trying to play god, thinking that we can still get the storm under control if we try a little harder. He is waiting for us to turn to him and turn ourselves over to him: "Lord God, help me out of my trouble. Calm this storm that is about to overtake me."

God desires to speak to our hurts. He comes and consoles us. He tells us he knows. He loves us and knows what we are going through. He speaks to the bitterness and calls forth forgiveness from us—forgiveness towards those who hurt us. He speaks to the sin and guilt and says, "I do not condemn you, go and sin no more." He speaks to the fear and says, "Peace be still." "Then they cried to the Lord in their trouble, and **he** brought them out from their distress." "He brought them to their desired haven."

He brings us to our desired haven.

What is your desired haven? To be at peace with yourself? To have peace with those with whom you are in relationship? To be able to love and be loved? God will bring you to your desired haven. Left to yourself, you will try to make it to the haven or try to build the haven and never manage it.

God gives us a haven. He brings us to it and establishes us in it. He heals us and delivers us. He makes things right. Will you believe him for that today?

God's haven is awaiting us. Jesus says, "I am come that you might have life and have it abundantly" (John 10:10). Our haven has already been prepared for us! And our Lord is inviting us to receive it. He is offering it. He is saying, "See I offer it to you." "Come to me all you who are weary and heavy laden and I will give you rest. Learn from me for I am humble of heart, and you will find rest for your souls" (Matthew 11:29-30). "Learn from me! And you will receive rest. You will come into your haven!" Our Lord is our haven. He brings us to himself. "He is our refuge and strength, a very present help in trouble" (Psalm 46:1).

I have gotten lost many times, especially driving, in the city and out. But I do not remember ever being lost when backpacking in the wilderness and in the mountains. I think that is because of what I know about the nature of wilderness and "the elements." I respect the wilderness. I cannot take it for granted. I have to pay attention.

How much more so with the Creator of the wilderness. How much more must we pay attention to the Guardian of our souls and cry out to him and listen to him. He knows the topography of our souls. He knows the mounds or mountains of bitterness that have built up. He knows the valley of disappointment and the pit of despair and the quicksand of unforgiveness and the storm of anger. He knows when a storm is about to develop and where it comes from. He knows that we are afraid of what we might do to ourselves as well as what others might do to us. He comes to us in the midst of raging storms within and without. He is ready to say, "Peace be still," and lead us to our desired haven. He wants to do that today! Will you let him?

10 God Raises Up The Needy To New Life!

He turns rivers into a desert,
 springs of water into thirsty ground,
a fruitful land into a salty waste,
 because of the wickedness of its inhabitants.
He turns a desert into pools of water,
 a parched land into springs of water.
And there he lets the hungry live,
 and they establish a town to live in;
they sow fields, and plant vineyards,
 and get a fruitful yield.
By his blessing they multiply greatly,
 and he does not let their cattle decrease.
When they are diminished and brought low
 through oppression, trouble, and sorrow,
he pours contempt on princes
 and makes them wander in trackless wastes;
but he raises up the needy out of distress,
 and makes their families like flocks.
The upright see it and are glad;
 and all wickedness stops its mouth.
Let those who are wise give heed to these things,
 and consider the steadfast love of the Lord. (Psalm
  107:33-43)

In these verses, we are told how God operates. God, at times, will reverse aspects of our lives. Our situation is of a particular kind, and God will turn things around so that our situation is of a different and opposite kind. At one time, he "turns rivers into a desert, springs of water into thirsty ground, a fruitful land into a salty waste," and at another, he "turns a desert into pools of water, a parched land into springs of water."

Sometimes we will focus on our situation and fret about it. God wants us to turn from concentrating on our situation and concentrate on him and his will for us, because he can reverse our situation.

There are reasons given in the text for the reversals that God brings about. He turns "a fruitful land into a salty waste, because of the wickedness of its inhabitants." On the other hand, for the hungry he turns "a desert into pools of water," and he lets the hungry live there and "sow fields, and plant vineyards, and get a fruitful yield." Not only that, but when they are "diminished and brought low through oppression, trouble, and sorrow" (and this happens because they still live in a world of evil), "he pours contempt on princes and makes them wander in trackless wastes; but he raises up the needy out of distress, and makes their families like flocks."

Mary, the mother of Jesus, sings about this way of God:

> He has shown strength with his arm;
>> he has scattered the proud in the thoughts of
>> their hearts.
> He has brought down the powerful from their
>> thrones, and lifted up the lowly;
>> he has filled the hungry with good things,
>> and sent the rich away empty. (Luke 1:51-
>> 53)

Jesus also teaches this: "All who exalt themselves will be humbled, and all who humble themselves will be exalted" (Matthew 23:12). The world may operate another way, but this is the way God operates!

I know how the world treats the needy. The world overlooks, judges and takes advantage of the needy. However, God is greater than this situation of sin, and God has overcome the world through Jesus Christ. Therefore, I need to listen to what God does. Sometimes we will spend much time on how bad the world is and not enough time on how great God is. I want to know the great things that God does for the needy because I am needy.

If we do not see ourselves as needy, then apparently we are in the other group, the "princes," those that rule. They have to be brought down to find out that they are needy. And any of us can get to a place where we think we rule. Our kingdom may be small, but what we have, we are in charge of. In our hearts, we may say, "I am the ruler of my domain"—whatever that domain is! God in his love for us—when we are trying to play god—will bring us down, so that he can truly raise us up. God raises up the needy!

Who are the needy?

Jesus says, "Blessed are you who are needy, for yours is the kingdom of God." The world says, "Blessed are you who are rich, for the earth is yours." Jesus speaks the truth against the lie. In fact Jesus says even more: "Woe to you who are rich, for you have received your consolation. Woe to you who are full now, for you will be hungry" (Luke 6:20-25). It is better to be needy, no matter how much money we have. It is better to know we need God, that we cannot live without him, that we cannot live by bread alone and that we need every word that comes from the mouth of God.

Do you know you are needy today? Do you know that you are not strong in yourself, that you can only be strong with the strength of God and the power of his might? Do you know that without him you can do nothing, and that without him you will fail? Do you know that you can do all things through him who strengthens you? Do you know that however you have needed him in the past and however he has helped you in the past, you still need him today? Do you know that today you need his wisdom and guidance and power; you cannot truly live without it?

We have recognized some of the things that we get enslaved to: fear, desire, hurt, guilt, etc. We are reminded again and again how much we need God to deliver us out of bondages from which we are unable to free ourselves. We can come to God today as needy people and know that he is present to raise us up. We cannot come thinking that we can bargain with God and tell God why we think he ought to raise us up. It is as needy people that we approach God.

You may be feeling much weakness of faith today. You are needy! You may be feeling the weight of disappointments, great and small. You are needy! You may find yourself acting out of the same wounds that you have acted out of so many times before. You are needy! You may have fallen for the same temptation again. You are needy!

There is good news for you: God raises up needy people! Come to him, therefore, that he may raise you up. Seek and you will find. Knock and the door to new life will be opened.

What is it like to be raised up?

This question is important because there are some major misunderstandings regarding God prospering us. These misunderstandings cause all kinds of confusion and frustration.

When I go to the doctor, I go hoping that he won't tell me something is wrong. However, if he finds something wrong I certainly want him to tell me! I do not want him to paint a rosy picture of my condition because he doesn't want to make me feel bad. Sometimes, when I hear people talk about God, it sounds like they think God is simply there to say good things over their lives. He is there to tell them what he is going to do for them and how everything will be better when he gives them what they wanted but were unable to obtain. They seem to think that God is there to add to their lives what *they* think would be good for them—that is what God is for. They may even "name it and claim it." But then they are disappointed at what God is not doing. The problem is that they are wrong about our relationship with God. He is not like a magician who pulls a rabbit out of a hat so that we now have a rabbit we didn't have before.

Our relationship with God is more like our relationship to a doctor. We come in need. It hurts somewhere in our lives. We do not know the diagnosis, the prognosis or the treatment. We are so very needy. We say, "Doctor, tell me why it hurts and what can be done about it." And we say to God, "God, why is my life the way it is? Why are things falling apart? Why is my soul cast down within me? Why do you seem far away from me, God? Why do I groan and sigh? Lord God, help me!"

Now, if we will listen, God, our great physician, will speak to us! He will tell us about our condition. It may not be at all what we expect. When I went to see my skin doctor about a concern I had, I kept pointing to a sore on my forehead. He, however, kept looking at something on the side of my face that I had not seen before. I urged him to take a closer look at the blemish on my forehead. He told me it was nothing to be concerned about, although if it would make me feel better he would remove it. What he was concerned about, and what turned out to be a skin cancer, was on the side of my face. Sometimes we go to God thinking we know our problem, and God points to a completely different area of our lives.

God starts showing us our condition. It is our condition that is causing so many problems. It is our sin sickness. God starts touching on things that we would rather not have him tampering with. God, our great and loving physician, then tells us that he has to do surgery. My doctor said it so simply and matter-of-factly: "We will cut that skin cancer out." God says, "That sin has to go. It is killing you, so it is going to have to die. You are going to have to die to that old life." "Unless a grain of wheat falls into the earth and dies, it remains just a single grain; but if it dies, it bears much fruit" (John 12:24).

What is it like to be raised up? It is like dying to the old and becoming alive to the new. It is like leaving behind the old life and walking into the new. It is like being lost and then being found, being dead and now alive. It is like having the cancer cut out and the doctor saying, "We got it all."

After surgery, there are instructions. It is important to follow the instructions. When I went back to have my stitches out, the doctor said, "You did a good job taking care of the wound." (I heard, "Well done, good and faithful servant.") I did not tell him that my wife, who is a nurse, had much to do with that.

God has instructions for us. Daily he instructs us, giving us direction so that the healing and the new life can continue. God's living and active word is a lamp unto our feet. We have spent much time listening to the lies of the world around us which got us lost. Now that we are found and made alive, it is time to listen to another voice, to hear the voice of the God who has raised us up. There is no where else to go. The God who has come to us in Jesus Christ has the words of eternal life. We are to listen to him and follow him.

Maybe you are saying, "His instructions are too hard. His words are too strong. I am afraid of what he has to say to me. He is touching on things in my life that I would rather not deal with. His diagnosis for my condition makes me tremble." My brother, my sister, where would you go? He has the words of eternal life, and he has the cure. Receive his instructions through the Scriptures, within the community of faith and in prayer with the help of the Holy Spirit. He has come that you might have life and have it abundantly. There is no turning back now.

Rebuilding Our Lives

11 God Gives Us What We Need To Rebuild

For Zion's sake I will not keep silent,
    and for Jerusalem's sake I will not rest,
until her vindication shines out like the dawn,
    and her salvation like a burning torch.
The nations shall see your vindication,
    and all the kings your glory;
and you shall be called by a new name
    that the mouth of the LORD will give.
You shall be a crown of beauty in the hand of
      the LORD,
    and a royal diadem in the hand of your
      God.
You shall no more be termed Forsaken,
    and your land shall no more be termed
      Desolate;
but you shall be called My Delight Is in Her,
    and your land Married;
for the LORD delights in you,
    and your land shall be married.
For as a young man marries a young woman,
    so shall your builder marry you,
and as the bridegroom rejoices over the bride,
    so shall your God rejoice over you.
      (Isaiah 62:1-5)

The prophet will not keep silent, either with God in prayer or with speaking to the people the prophetic word. The word he speaks is to those who have returned from exile. After seventy years in captivity in Babylon, God made a way for his people to return to their homeland, to Judea and Jerusalem and the temple. They walked 500 miles through wilderness and danger to get there, and when they came home they found Jerusalem destroyed along with the temple. They had to rebuild everything. They had been released from bondage to rebuild their lives.

When the Lord releases us from bondage, we step into freedom to take responsibility for our lives. As we do so, we often face the mess and brokenness that has always been there, but which we never fully admitted. We may begin to feel that—even though we have been released from whatever has bound us—we are forsaken and our situation is desolate. These people in our reading from Isaiah felt the same way. This word of the Lord speaks to people who have been freed from bondage, but now must rebuild what has broken down.

This is a word for people rebuilding their lives. It is good news for us. God gives us what we need to rebuild. The God who released us from bondage to rebuild our lives, is in our lives to build in and through us. God does so by giving us a new identity, a new stature and a new relationship.

God gives us a new identity.

"The nations shall see your vindication, and all the kings your glory; and you shall be called by a new name that the mouth of the LORD will give." Released from bondage, we are given a new identity. What we rebuild will not be what we were and had before. It will be a new thing that coincides with the new life we have in God. We are being made over anew. We are becoming new creations in Christ. The old is passing away and all is new in him. We are seeing things differently. We are learning a new way to live and operate. The Holy Spirit is enlightening the eyes of our hearts so that we look at the world and ourselves and our children and others differently.

It is important that we take up this new identity, that we let the Lord give us a new name. God is taking us out of an old way of perceiving things into a new life. The old life was filled with self-deception. This new life is filled with truth. We are becoming real about ourselves and about life and about God's purposes for us.

Those who are recovering from drug addiction often share that, in their addictive behavior, they spent much time looking for that person, place or thing that was going to make everything right. They lived with a magical view of the world rather than a realistic view. Rather than live life on life's terms they were constantly trying to find the magic wand. They may even have approached religion that way. Religion was tried as another magic wand. This experience, however, is not only the experience of those who have struggled with drug addictions, but all of us who have been held bound by any addiction or idolatry.

We lived with a false view of life and we built up what was a false identity. But now God has come to us in Christ Jesus to set us free from that which had us bound—our false dependencies—to serve the true and living God. He now gives us a new name to correspond to our new life and our new way of seeing things. We are learning to trust in the living God. We are learning to live life on life's terms in the power of the Holy Spirit. We are learning to face things today.

God is giving us a new identity!

God gives us a new stature.

"You shall be a crown of beauty in the hand of the LORD, and a royal diadem in the hand of your God. You shall no more be termed Forsaken, and your land shall no more be termed Desolate; but you shall be called My Delight Is in Her, and your land Married; for the LORD delights in you, and your land shall be married." When God releases us from bondage, we are given eyes to see what our bondage has produced. We start to see the waste and the destruction of our ways. Others, who have seen our dysfunction before we did, have been saying things about us. "She is destroying her life." "He is messing up." We have been called *forsaken* and our situation *desolate*.

Some of these people may have been members of our own family and former friends. But now that God has released us from bondage and continues to set us free, he gives us a new stature, so that those who used to say we were hopeless, will have to say, "God's delight is in her." See what God is doing in her life!

"You shall be called My Delight Is in Her, and your land Married; for the LORD delights in you, and your land shall be married." Someone has laid claim to you. People were saying, "No one wants him or her." They are now going to say, "They are married." They are not only wanted, but someone has a claim on them now. God has laid claim to us. God is raising us up. God is giving us a new stature. God is making something of our lives. I think of a brother in the Lord whose testimony was, "I used to be a predator, but now I am a productive citizen. God took me from a wasteland and made of me someone who could now give back to the community. People want what I have now." God gives us new stature! Thanks be to God.

God gives us a new relationship.

"For as a young man marries a young woman, so shall your builder marry you, and as the bridegroom rejoices over the bride, so shall your God rejoice over you." God gives us a new relationship. The one who releases us from bondage marries us. The one who now is present in our lives to build up our lives unites himself to us. And he rejoices over us.

God gives us a new relationship with himself. It used to be that our relationship with God was defined by distant requests of God when we got into a bad situation only to forget about God when things seemed more or less okay. Or our relationship with God consisted in going to God when we couldn't get what we wanted. We would go to God in what we called prayer—but which was more like wishful thinking—and ask God to give to us what we said we could not live without. "God I really want this, and it just isn't happening. I have tried so hard. God you have to do something for me."

We had not yet learned to want God's will. We did not know that our true blessing was in God's purpose for us. We sought his hands, not his face. We were interested in what he could do for us, not in who he was and what he willed. But now, God has released us from bondage in order that we might have a new kind of relationship with him, one that looks more like marriage than anything else we can humanly understand. This relationship is about him now. We are in love with him and what is on his heart.

There is something intimate and personal that comes with faithfulness and commitment. God has been faithful to us, and this faithfulness has called forth our commitment, like that of a man and woman face to face speaking the words of a pledge into each other's eyes, "For better, for worse, for richer, for poorer, in sickness and in health, to love and to cherish, until death parts us."

Paul likens the relationship between the church and Jesus to marriage. He quotes from Genesis: "For this reason a man will leave his father and mother and be joined to his wife, and the two will become one flesh." And then he says: "This is a great mystery, and I am applying it to Christ and the church" (Ephesians 5:31-32). In a Christian wedding service there is a point where the minister declares: "What God has joined together, let no one put asunder." In our relationship with God as well, nothing must get in the way. Like marriage, it is a whole self, whole life commitment. It demands our all.

God is our all in all. Without him we can do nothing. Are you married today? "Your builder shall marry you, and as the bridegroom rejoices over the bride, so shall your God rejoice over you." God your deliverer and the builder of your life shall marry you. Can you turn him down? He comes to rejoice over you as a bridegroom rejoices over his bride. And he is a faithful bridegroom. He will not leave you or forsake you.

You have tried various people, places and things, and they have let you down. God will never be unfaithful. "God remains faithful—for he cannot deny himself" (2 Timothy 2:13). God is faithful. God is love. Where else would you and I go for new life and the rebuilding of our lives, if not to God. He desires us. He wants us to turn to him again today—and receive from him.

12 Relearn To Rebuild

All the people gathered together into the square before the Water Gate. They told the scribe Ezra to bring the book of the law of Moses, which the LORD had given to Israel. Accordingly, the priest Ezra brought the law before the assembly, both men and women and all who could hear with understanding. This was on the first day of the seventh month. He read from it facing the square before the Water Gate from early morning until midday, in the presence of the men and the women and those who could understand; and the ears of all the people were attentive to the book of the law. And Ezra opened the book in the sight of all the people, for he was standing above all the people; and when he opened it, all the people stood up. Then Ezra blessed the LORD, the great God, and all the people answered, "Amen, Amen," lifting up their hands. Then they bowed their heads and worshiped the LORD with their faces to the ground. So they read from the book, from the law of God, with interpretation. They gave the sense, so that the people understood the reading. And Nehemiah, who was the governor, and Ezra the priest and scribe, and the Levites who taught the people said to all the people, "This day is holy to the LORD your God; do not mourn or weep." For all the people wept when they heard the words of the law. Then he said to them, "Go your way, eat the fat and drink sweet wine and send portions of them to those for whom nothing is prepared, for this day is holy to our LORD; and do not be grieved, for the joy of the LORD is your strength." (Nehemiah 8:1-3, 5-6, 8-10)

The people of Israel had returned home from exile. They had entered into the struggle of rebuilding their homes and the city of Jerusalem and the temple. They had to rebuild even as their enemies tried to stop them. We have been released to rebuild, but not everyone wants us to rebuild. We are under attack both from within and from without.

In addition, we do not necessarily know how to rebuild. Just because we have been released from bondage does not mean we are ready to rebuild our lives. About half of those released from prison in the state of Illinois end up back in prison in about three years. Clearly being set free is not all that is needed. Those who are released from prison, need a community that is prepared to receive them back and support them in becoming productive citizens. They need training; they need jobs; they need a new perspective on life.

We can be released from bondage to addiction and find our way back to the addiction we were released from or into a new addiction. We can be released from bondage to sin, to a particular sin, and be right back into it or come up with another "sin of choice." We can get free of a situation of abuse only to put ourselves back into another situation of abuse. We can be the abuser and ask for forgiveness and be given a new chance only to fall back into abusive ways. Something else has to happen to us beyond our initially being set free!

When God sets us free to rebuild our lives, we need his teaching. The text at the beginning of this chapter refers to the law of Moses being read and interpreted to the people. The law or "Torah" referred to here may be the book of Leviticus or it may be the first five books of the Bible. Whatever books of the the Bible are included here, it is instruction that is being passed on to the people.

If we have been released from bondage to rebuild our lives, then we have some relearning to do. We cannot simply go back to what we learned before, which got us into bondage. ("If we do what we have always done, we will get what we have always got.") We must relearn and therefore be re-taught—now from God's teaching. We must relearn to rebuild!

God's instruction is for everyone.

"All the people gathered together into the square before the Water Gate." They gathered in the place where everyone could come. There were places for the priests, places for men, and other places for women and Gentiles. But they gathered where even those who were considered unclean or defiled could gather. Men, women and children heard the Lord's instruction. "He read from it facing the square before the Water Gate from early morning until midday, in the presence of the men and the women and those who could understand; and the ears of all the people were attentive to the book of the law."

My sister, my brother, God's teaching is for you. Do not let anyone or anything imply otherwise. It does not matter where you have been or what you have been into. God has instruction that will change *your* life. He has guidance just for you, for your situation and for your relationships. You do not need to keep doing the same old things that have been tearing down the walls of your new life, even as you are trying to build them up. Get God's instruction. It is for you.

God's instruction is to be sought after.

"All the people gathered together into the square before the Water Gate. They told the scribe Ezra to bring the book of the law of Moses, which the LORD had given to Israel." It is the people who called for the instruction. They, in essence, said, "We want Bible study. We want teaching. We want and need God's word."

Oh, that people of faith today would have such earnestness about God's word! "The ears of all the people were attentive to the book of the law." And when Ezra opened the book of teaching, we read that "all the people stood up." There was honor and respect for God's word. And the people "bowed their heads and worshiped the LORD with their faces to the ground." There is submission to the living God as the word of God is about to be read. God's instruction is to be sought after, and we are to listen to it with ears that are attentive and lives that are ready to submit.

My brother, my sister, would you like to see positive change in your life? Would you like to know what it is like for the living God to rebuild your life? Would you like to know the kinds of relationships that God has for you and how to be in relationship? Do you want to know from God how to build a marriage or how to parent children? Would you like to know from God how to view your job or how to handle your finances? Would you like to know how your attitudes can change and how those destructive forces can be dealt with? Do you want to know how you can experience healing in your life and be set free from what still has you bound? Seek after God's guidance. Seek God's instruction in the community of God's people where the word is preached and taught and shared. Seek after it in prayer and with your whole heart.

Many Christians have found great help being in a Bible study group, especially a small group where people are able to share and pray. Formal Bible teaching is important, but small groups give opportunity for sharing with others. We are able to communicate our needs to one another as well as what we believe God is saying to us or doing in our lives. It is important that in such groups the participants pray for each other and together seek after God's instruction.

God's instruction must be applied.

"So they read from the book, from the law of God, with interpretation. They gave the sense, so that the people understood the reading."

They read with interpretation. The sense of what was being read was given. In other words, they broke it down so that it could be applied to their lives. When people come together for Bible study, they often spend time simply interpreting the meaning of the words. They ask questions about what the words meant when they were first written down or spoken. They do this so that they might apply the words to their lives today.

What good is it to us, if God tells us to have no other gods before him, when, after hearing it, we continue to make something in our lives more important than God? What good is it, if children hear God's instructions to obey their parents only to defy authority? How are our relationships helped, if God tells us not to commit adultery, and we rationalize ourselves into a relationship that God did not have for us? Where is there new life for us, when we are instructed by God to be merciful, and we continue to judge our brother?

God gives us instruction to love one another, to share the word with one another, to sing spiritual songs and to bring healing to others in the name of Christ. God's instruction is life-giving. It is for those who have been released and are rebuilding their lives. God's instruction must be applied!

God's instruction must be received with joy.

> And Nehemiah, who was the governor, and Ezra the priest and scribe, and the Levites who taught the people said to all the people, "This day is holy to the LORD your God; do not mourn or weep." For all the people wept when they heard the words of the law. Then he said to them, "Go your way, eat the fat and drink sweet wine and send portions of them to those for whom nothing is prepared, for this day is holy to our LORD; and do not be grieved, for the joy of the LORD is your strength."

God's word can bring weeping. We can grieve the many years we did not listen to the living God. We can mourn our sins. But what holds us up, even when we are having such feelings, is the joy of the Lord. "For the joy of the LORD is your strength."

At times when we receive the word of God into our lives and apply it, we receive and apply it with tears. There is both weeping and joy at the same time, but the joy of the Lord is our strength. The joy of the Lord enables us to hear even the hard word of truth that God speaks to us. The joy of the Lord upholds us, even as God is disciplining us by his word. The joy of the Lord is our strength as we carry out the word.

God calls us to actions that we cannot do on our own. Without the strength of God, there are some changes that we cannot make. But God gives us the necessary strength, and the joy of the Lord keeps us while we are going through difficult transformations.

Are you having to make a change in your life today? Maybe the Lord is calling you from something that has been an idol. Perhaps the Lord is commanding you to let go of a particular way of operating or a relationship. Perhaps the Lord is calling you to step out of your comfort zone into the new thing that he has for you. There is no moving on with the Lord until you are obedient. The joy of the Lord will be your strength as you take those steps of obedience. However, disobedience can rob you of that joy and strength.

We must make decisions about God's word and where it will be in our lives. Where is God's word in your life? I will use the image of a Bible on a shelf. The Bible, in this illustration, is a symbol of the word of God, the word of God being much greater since by God's word all was created and Jesus is God's Word incarnate. Imagine that you have a Bible on a shelf.

On what shelf is it? Is it on the bottom shelf or the top shelf? What else is on the shelf with the Bible? Is there a self-help book? How to make your first million dollars? Books representing various interests? A pornographic magazine or video? Are there violent video games? Is there something hidden behind the objects on the shelf? Something in your life you don't want anyone else to know about—but which God knows about? What is on your shelf? What do you reach for? What do you regularly take down from the shelf?

What are the words that you habitually reach for to make a life for yourself? What messages do you think will bring you life or help you get by? Where is God's word in your life today? Where are you getting your instruction?

The people told Ezra to bring the book of God's instructions to them. God's instructions are to be sought after. They are to be desired more than gold.

> The law of the LORD is perfect,
>> reviving the soul;
> the decrees of the LORD are sure,
>> making wise the simple;
> the precepts of the LORD are right,
>> rejoicing the heart;
> the commandment of the LORD is clear,
>> enlightening the eyes;
> the fear of the LORD is pure,
>> enduring forever;
> the ordinances of the LORD are true
>> and righteous altogether.
> More to be desired are they than gold,
>> even much fine gold;
> sweeter also than honey,
>> and drippings of the honeycomb.
> Moreover by them is your servant warned;
>> in keeping them there is great reward.
>> (Psalm 19)

Reach out for the instruction of the Lord. He changes our lives through his teaching. Receive it. Apply it. In obeying his word there is great reward.

13 We Start To Rebuild When We Start To Follow

When the days drew near for him to be taken up, he set his face to go to Jerusalem. And he sent messengers ahead of him. On their way they entered a village of the Samaritans to make ready for him; but they did not receive him, because his face was set toward Jerusalem. When his disciples James and John saw it, they said, "Lord, do you want us to command fire to come down from heaven and consume them?" But he turned and rebuked them. Then they went on to another village. As they were going along the road, someone said to him, "I will follow you wherever you go." And Jesus said to him, "Foxes have holes, and birds of the air have nests; but the Son of Man has nowhere to lay his head." To another he said, "Follow me." But he said, "Lord, first let me go and bury my father." But Jesus said to him, "Let the dead bury their own dead; but as for you, go and proclaim the kingdom of God." Another said, "I will follow you, Lord; but let me first say farewell to those at my home." Jesus said to him, "No one who puts a hand to the plow and looks back is fit for the kingdom of God." (Luke 9:51-62)

Jesus is going to Jerusalem where, as he already told his disciples, he will "give his life to liberate many people" (Mark 10:45, CEB). He moves with determination as he enters the last phase of his mission. He "sets his face" towards Jerusalem where he will find confrontation, suffering and death. Where he is going and what he is about to endure makes some draw back from him. "And he sent messengers ahead of him. On their way they entered a village of the Samaritans to make ready for him; but they did not receive him, because his face was set toward Jerusalem." What he is about to do makes others nervous. "When his disciples James and John saw it, they said, 'Lord, do you want us to command fire to come down from heaven and consume them?'" Did they even know what they were saying? "But he turned and rebuked them."

As Jesus was moving toward Jerusalem there were still some who considered following him—three "wannabe" disciples. They are drawn to Jesus. They may or may not have known where Jesus was going and what he was about to endure, but something had happened that attracted them to Jesus. Perhaps it was his teaching with authority or his healings or his casting out evil spirits. Perhaps they had experienced being healed or delivered.

Being delivered from something that has had you bound can make you a "wannabe" follower of Jesus. It doesn't necessarily make you a follower. God makes the sun shine and the rain fall on the just and the unjust, the follower and the non-follower. God will heal, and God will deliver. But Jesus warns us against merely sweeping things clean when we have gotten delivered from some evil and then leaving our life empty. Otherwise, he says, seven demons worst than the first will find the empty place and fill it.

We may have been released from bondage to rebuild our lives, but we truly start to rebuild when we start following

Jesus. Do you want to rebuild your life? Do you want to experience the new life growing in you? Then follow Jesus! Following Jesus means keeping Jesus in front of us. It means that with our whole lives we are going to follow him and in so doing see a new life built up, not one of our own making.

Perhaps you are thinking about becoming a follower of Jesus. Perhaps you are a follower who needs to be reminded what it means to follow. Whether we are a "wannabe follower" or a follower needing a reminder, there are some things we need to know.

Following Jesus means being on a journey.

"As they were going along the road, someone said to him, 'I will follow you wherever you go.'" This person sounds like he is ready to follow. He says he is ready to go anywhere. But sometimes we are carried away with our feelings. Jesus has to bring clarity to our minds: "And Jesus said to him, 'Foxes have holes, and birds of the air have nests; but the Son of Man has nowhere to lay his head.'" If you follow me, you will not be able to set up house for yourself. You will not be able to secure your own nice nest or nest egg! You will be on a journey. At a moment's notice you may have to change direction as your guide gives you further instructions.

Most people live by their whims, lusts, prejudices, impulses, hurts, grievances, as well as ways of thinking which are built up from their hurts, grievances, lusts and impulses. The followers of Jesus, however, while experiencing all these things, are finding themselves being lead. They are on a journey. They do not know what tomorrow will bring. They do not know what Jesus has next. What they do know is that they must be ready, willing, open, movable, and listening.

Following Jesus means Jesus is in front.

"To another he said, 'Follow me.' But he said, 'Lord, first let me go and bury my father.' But Jesus said to him, 'Let the dead bury their own dead; but as for you, go and proclaim the kingdom of God.'" Jesus calls. We respond. Jesus clarifies. Jesus calls us to follow him. We respond with how we see ourselves doing that. Jesus clarifies what it really means to follow him.

There is always the temptation to put something in front of Jesus. What we are tempted to put in front of him, in our minds, is always important—a child, spouse, parent, girl friend, boy friend, health, sickness, death. ("Lord, *first* let me go and bury my father.") Jesus' response to our very important issues may seem harsh. Nothing must come before God's reign. Following Jesus means he is first. He is before all conventions of society, all other expectations on our lives, before family and all other relationships. The follower must be attentive to what Jesus is saying in his or her life before anything else. Jesus' response to this wannabe follower: "As for you, go and proclaim the kingdom of God." Above all, the followers of Jesus have something to proclaim and nothing better get in the way of this task that has been laid on us.

Following Jesus means not looking back.

"Another said, 'I will follow you, Lord; but let me first say farewell to those at my home.' Jesus said to him, 'No one who puts a hand to the plow and looks back is fit for the kingdom of God.'" Following Jesus means not looking back. At the point of making a decision, we are often tempted to look back. I have seen this time and time again over the years. Individuals will glance back as they are getting close to making a decision to follow

Jesus. They will start to think about what they are going to give up. They will think about what they will have to do. "I will have to forgive that person, if I decide to follow Jesus. I will have to make amends." They find themselves in a struggle between what is ahead and what is behind, between the old life and the new.

Jesus speaks a word to those who are in such a struggle. It is a loving word, calling them to decide. "No one who puts a hand to the plow and looks back is fit for the kingdom of God." When we look back we demonstrate that we cannot decide whether to let God rule over our lives or go back to something or someone else. I do not know much about plowing, but I imagine that looking back while plowing could produce a very crooked row. If you and I take our eyes off Jesus who is always in front of us, we will lose our way.

This word also reminds us that there are two temptations that face us when we are following Jesus: the temptation to keep questioning what we are leaving behind and the temptation to ask how straight is our row. We can keep looking back to see if we are missing out on something, or we can keep looking back to make sure we are doing all right. Either way these temptations will side-track us. Checking out what we are missing can stop us from following. Continually checking to see how well we are doing can drive us to despair.

St. Paul writes of leaving the past behind. He presses on for the upward call of God in Christ Jesus his Lord! My brother, my sister, are you on a journey today? Who is in front of you? Are you looking forward? Are you saying, "I have decided to follow Jesus?" Perhaps God has touched you in a healing way. Perhaps God has delivered you from something that held you in bondage. You are released, but there are now steps to take. Do you want to rebuild your life? Do you want to grow into a new life? You are tired of going to God when you are in trouble only to fall back into the same traps. You haven't been building anything. You haven't been on a journey. It is time to decide to *follow* Jesus!

14 Rebuilding Through Obedience

And the LORD your God will make you abundantly prosperous in all your undertakings, in the fruit of your body, in the fruit of your livestock, and in the fruit of your soil. For the LORD will again take delight in prospering you, just as he delighted in prospering your ancestors, when you obey the LORD your God by observing his commandments and decrees that are written in this book of the law, because you turn to the LORD your God with all your heart and with all your soul. Surely, this commandment that I am commanding you today is not too hard for you, nor is it too far away. It is not in heaven, that you should say, "Who will go up to heaven for us, and get it for us so that we may hear it and observe it?" Neither is it beyond the sea, that you should say, "Who will cross to the other side of the sea for us, and get it for us so that we may hear it and observe it?" No, the word is very near to you; it is in your mouth and in your heart for you to observe. (Deuteronomy 30:9-14)

I imagine these words read to the people of Israel who were released from exile and bondage in Babylon and have returned to Jerusalem and Judea. They have been released to rebuild their homes and city and temple. They hear these words as a word of promise from the book of

Deuteronomy: "The LORD your God will make you abundantly prosperous in all your undertakings." That prosperity includes the fruit of their body—they will have children and a family. It includes the fruit of their livestock—they will have a livelihood, and the fruit of their soil—they will eat well.

God's intention is to prosper us in the rebuilding of our lives. We have been released from bondage for this purpose. God wants to prosper you my sister, my brother. He is ready to do it right now—no matter what you are facing, no matter what you are dealing with in your life. God prospers us even in the midst of an evil and broken world. The Israelites who had been released from bondage and returned from captivity still had to face hostility, confusion and discord. The God who prospered them did so in the midst of many hardships that they faced. God prospered them even as they were being attacked. He prospered their building and their battle. They had to fight off enemies even as they were rebuilding the walls of Jerusalem. We, also, are waging war against powers of darkness even as we build the new life God has provided for us. God prospers us in the thick of the battle.

Jesus speaks about prosperity in the midst of trials:

> Jesus said, "Truly I tell you, there is no one who has left house or brothers or sisters or mother or father or children or fields, for my sake and for the sake of the good news, who will not receive a hundredfold now in this age - houses, brothers and sisters, mothers and children, and fields, with persecutions - and in the age to come eternal life." (Mark 10:29-30)

We may want to ignore the words "with persecutions" in Jesus' words, but we do so at our own peril. Life on life's terms means that we face the reality of evil and temptation in the midst of our daily lives even as our lives are being built up in Christ.

The prospering that God does in our lives happens in the midst of struggle, hardship, heartache, and at times, disease, death of loved ones and broken relationships. And yet God does prosper us. God restores our relationships, builds up marriages and families, blesses our children, gives us the body of Christ, the family of God, gives us the Holy Spirit and gifts of the Spirit. God gives us a ministry and a purpose in life.

I do not want to trade the prospering work of God in my life for the promises of the devil. I do not want to trade the narrow, hard road that leads to life for the broad, easy road that leads to destruction. I do not want to trade God's word for the world's temptations. The lights and glamour and riches of the world do not—by themselves—make anyone happy, nor do positions of power. You can have all these things and still have your marriage end in divorce, your children turn against you, lose your friends, and get caught up in addictions, obsessions and sins of one kind or another that steadily destroy you, bit by bit robbing you of the ability to love.

God is ready to prosper us and to do so right now in the midst of whatever trials we face. Maybe we are like those Israelites who, having been released from captivity and having returned home, faced all kinds of destruction. The city of Jerusalem was demolished, the temple was no more, and homes were destroyed. As it was for them, we now face enemies who do not want us to rebuild. There are those who do not like the change that we are undergoing. We do not enter into the same kinds of activities with them. There are some we do not hang with anymore. There are those close to us who have been entangled with our past, our false dependencies and addictions. They are not sure they can adjust to the change they encounter in us. They have problems with us, and they are a source of testing and temptation. It is important to understand what they are going through without judging them. The real battle is spiritual. We are not up against flesh and blood but against spiritual forces of darkness.

In the midst of all this, God promises to prosper us. What are you having to face today? What are the kinds of things that have been coming against you? Know this, God can start prospering you today, even while forces are coming against you, even while people are speaking evil against you, even while people you work with do not understand you, even while there is turmoil in your home. God can start prospering you today! He wants to do so. He is ready! God has released you in order to prosper you. He is ready to do for you what you have been unable to do for yourself. But here is the key: Obey!

> The LORD your God will make you abundantly prosperous in all your undertakings...when you obey the LORD your God by observing his commandments and decrees that are written in this book of the law, because you turn to the LORD your God with all your heart and with all your soul.

There is a very important word here—*when*. As in "when you obey the LORD your God by observing his commandments and decrees...because you turn to the LORD your God with all your heart and with all your soul." God will prosper you when you obey. Our lives are being rebuilt as we obey God.

We turn to God in order to obey him.

We can only begin to obey God when we turn to God "with all our heart and with all our soul." We do not begin the journey of obedience until we turn to the Lord, and we do not turn to the Lord except with our whole self. The rebuilding of our lives begins when we start obeying the God we have turned to with our whole being.

Jesus tells the story of the "Prodigal Son" which is also called the story of the "Waiting Father." The younger of two sons goes to his father and, in essence, says, "I cannot wait until you're dead. Give me my inheritance now." His father gives him his portion of the inheritance and he goes out and squanders it on partying, prostitutes and "loose living." He ends up destitute, living in a place far from home, and hired out to feed pigs that eat better than he. He finally comes to his senses and decides he would do better as one of his father's servants than continuing in his present situation. He decides to go back not as a son but to ask his father if he would hire him. The story ends with the father running out to meet him, putting a robe on him, a ring on his finger, calling neighbors together to celebrate and having a big party. The father whose actions are an example of God's love proclaims that his son who was lost is now found and that he who was dead is now alive.

What we notice about the son who has lived a life of rebellion and disobedience is that he does not come back to a life of obedience until he turns back to his father. He has to turn back and come home. His whole self has to return. He cannot say, "Part of me will go to my father, and part of me will remain here to see if things might eventually work out." He has to return with his whole self, placing himself before his father, and awaiting his father's decision. Of course, he ends up prospering with his father, and that prosperity begins immediately. The point, however, is that we can only know God's prospering us when we are in relationship with God as our Father. It is as we come into the life of obedience that we receive from our Father his good gifts. Our prosperity is in the will of God, not outside God's will. Therefore, we must return to the Lord our God with our whole self in order to begin obeying him.

Even today we can turn to him. If we have drifted away, if we have run away, even now we can return. He calls us to come to him and receive from him. "Every generous act of giving, with every perfect gift, is from above, coming down from the Father of lights" (James 1:17). Come to him! Receive from him. Return with your whole self to obey him. We turn to God in order to obey him, and in the shelter of his will, we prosper!

God helps us with our obeying.

> Surely, this commandment that I am commanding you today is not too hard for you, nor is it too far away. It is not in heaven, that you should say, "Who will go up to heaven for us, and get it for us so that we may hear it and observe it?" Neither is it beyond the sea, that you should say, "Who will cross to the other side of the sea for us, and get it for us so that we may hear it and observe it?" No, the word is very near to you; it is in your mouth and in your heart for you to observe.

God's commandment is not too hard. It is not too far away. It is very near. See how gracious and merciful God is to us. He makes it so that his commandment is not too hard, nor too far away. God makes it so that we are able to obey. "For the love of God is this, that we obey his commandments. And his commandments are not burdensome, for whatever is born of God conquers the world. And this is the victory that conquers the world, our faith" (1 John 5:3-4). For those who have been born of God through Jesus Christ, who have returned to the Lord and received the Holy Spirit, God's commands are not burdensome "for whatever is born of God conquers the world." In our relationship with God, we are learning to trust in God for the power we need to do what God calls us to do!

God's commandment is not too hard. God gives us the guidance and power of the Holy Spirit. What is God calling you to do today? Is God calling you to a particular work of love toward another person, a work of forgiveness and mercy? Is he calling you to acknowledge your need or to confess your sin? Is he calling you to repent, to turn away from something that is not of him? Whatever it is, he gives you the power to do what he calls you to do! Is there a ministry he calls you into, an act of serving? Has he already given you something to do that you have been drawing back from in fear? My brother, my sister, know this: God gives you the power to do what he calls you to do. God's commandment is not too hard. Therefore, be obedient and not rebellious. He will help you. Trust him at his word. What he commands you to do is not too hard for him, working in and through you.

Nor is God's command too far away! God's "word is very near to you; it is in your mouth and in your heart for you to observe." God's word is near you because he puts it in your heart so that you can speak it from your mouth. We must be mindful of two things: (1) God speaks to us in such a manner that we are able to hear. (2) We must obey the word that is near rather than choosing the one far away.

First, God speaks in such a manner that we can hear. God is determined to get through to us. God comes to us where we can hear him—in our hearts. In our consciences, his "still small voice" speaks. Only our refusal and persistence in being rebellious keeps us from hearing the Lord. God wants us to hear him! God makes himself known!

Second, obey the word that is near rather than choosing the one far away. We receive many words of command and direction from the Lord in the course of a life time. Sometimes we will rationalize ourselves away from obedience by attending to yesterday's word in order to avoid today's word. Obey the word that is near rather than choosing the one far away.

For example, let us say that we are in an adulterous relationship, but instead of repenting and obeying the Lord, we talk about how we always keep the commandment "not to kill." We focus on the thing that is not at issue in order to ignore the thing that is. Or we go regularly to worship services as a replacement for forgiving someone. We "praise" God instead of reconciling with a sister or brother. We do this or that good deed, instead of coming to God with the present sin or obsession. We do the ministry we have become comfortable with instead of obeying God and stepping out into the ministry he now calls us to. We choose a word far away, rather than the one God has been putting in our face. God keeps putting something on our heart. We keep trying to chase it away by bringing up the far-away word. Obey the word that is near rather than choosing the one far away.

God's word is not too hard nor is it too far away. Let us be real here. Sometimes we experience the word as hard and as far away. The word says that it is not **too** hard and not **too** far away. It may seem hard because of the flesh, because of our pride, because of our desires, but it is not too hard because God gives us his Spirit. There is power available. It may seem far away because we are rebellious and push it away, but it is not too far away because God keeps bringing it near.

What is God saying to you today? He keeps speaking to us! Receive his word. Obey his word. It is not too hard, nor too far away.

15 God Has A Purpose For Your Life

Now the word of the LORD came to me saying,

> "Before I formed you in the womb I knew
> you,
>> and before you were born I consecrated
>> you;
> I appointed you a prophet to the nations."
>> Then I said, "Ah, LORD GOD! Truly I do
>> not know how to speak, for I am only
>> a boy."

But the LORD said to me,

> "Do not say, 'I am only a boy'; for you shall
> go to all to whom I send you,
>> and you shall speak whatever I com-
>> mand you,
> Do not be afraid of them,
>> for I am with you to deliver you, says
>> the LORD."

Then the LORD put out his hand and touched my mouth; and the LORD said to me,

> "Now I have put my words in your mouth.
> See, today I appoint you over nations and
>> over kingdoms,
>> to pluck up and to pull down,
>> to destroy and to overthrow,
>> to build and to plant." (Jeremiah 1:4-10)

Every human being has a purpose for his or her life that comes from God. God calls us to be and to do something. We are not left to hang around wondering what we are to do. There is a calling on each person's life. We are to rebuild our lives with a purpose.

Even right now every one of us can identify some of our vocations. All of us are called to be children of God. Whether we are right now living out that calling and purpose, we are called to be children of God. If we have children, we are called to be parents. If we have a husband or wife, we are called to nurture and build that relationship. If we are single, we are called to exercise our gifts in serving others in the unencumbered "freedom" of the single and celibate life. If we have a job, we are called to do it to the glory of God. If we are without a job, we are called to trust in God with patience. If we see our neighbor in need, we are to respond in love. We are called to pray. We are called by God to be in the fellowship of the saints. We are under call by God to obey his word.

God has a purpose for each of us. There are a variety of purposes, just as their are a variety of gifts. We do not all have the same gifts, and we do not all have the exact same purpose. Jeremiah was called by God to be a "prophet to the nations." Few have that calling, but each of us have our own calling by which we find fulfillment in life.

God has known, consecrated and appointed you.

"Before I formed you in the womb I knew you, and before you were born I consecrated you; I appointed you a prophet to the nations." Before God formed you in the womb, God appointed you for a purpose. God has something for you to do that fits who he created you to be! You and I don't "just exist." We exist for a purpose. We are not here to simply try out things as if life were like a potluck supper where we keep going back to experience another dish of food. People who know they have a purpose from God do not get up in the morning and ask what kind of experience they are going to try out today. Nor do they get up and decide how they can survive. Their first words are not, "How am I going to get through today?" but rather, "Lord, what do you have for me today? In whatever I face, show me your purpose. Show me what I am to do!"

God has direction and goals for our lives. God knew us before we were conceived. He consecrated us. That is, he set us apart for a particular purpose even before we were born. We came into this world appointed by God to fulfill a purpose God designed us for! We may have wasted time caught up in other things, but now we have come back to him and to our purpose. It is good to know that God has a purpose for us right now, whatever our past has been.

God is with you to help you perform your purpose.

"Then I said, 'Ah, Lord GOD! Truly I do not know how to speak, for I am only a boy.' But the LORD said to me, 'Do not say, 'I am only a boy'; for you shall go to all to whom I send you, and you shall speak whatever I command you, Do not be afraid of them, for I am with you to deliver you, says the LORD.'" When we start to realize our purpose, when we begin to hear God's call, we generally will say, "You can't really mean me. Not for this. I am not prepared. I do not know how to do that. I am only this or that." I am too young. I am too old. I am too shy. I am too bold. I am too controlling. I am too submissive. I've got issues. I have self-esteem problems. I have the wrong temperament, at which point we usually can point out someone else that we think would be better at it than us, as Moses did at the burning bush: "Lord, send my brother. He speaks much better than I do." The Lord said to Moses what he said to Jeremiah and what he says to us: "Do not be afraid...for I am with you."

God is with us. God gives us something to do that we cannot do without him and then promises to be with us. Our only focus needs to be him and his will for us. The doing of it, he will provide for with his presence and power. God is with us to help us do what he has called us to do.

Are you a parent? Are you called to raise up children today? Do you feel that it is too big for you, too many things can go wrong, and you could make a mess of it? You may feel that left to yourself you cannot do it, but God says, "I have called you to be a parent, and I am with you to perform it." The calling God has placed on us—to rebuild our lives, our marriages, our families, our communities, our churches—he has not left us to perform on our own. He is with us to guide and empower us.

The flip side is that he is not with us to do anything else. Many of us are in the habit of thinking about experiences we would like to have, places we would like to go, things we would like to do, and then making decisions about these thoughts. Then we go to God. We say to God, "God I wonder if this idea that I have been spending time on could possibly be your will?" The problem is that we did not start with God's will or with seeking God's will. We get to God's will last. We come to God and say, "Lord, this thing I want to do, that came to me when I was anxious and trying to see my way to fix something, or that I simply had a hankering for—is there some way this could become your will?"

Jesus tells us that this approach is backwards. Jesus tells us that there is really only one thing we need do and that is to seek God's kingdom. It is from that seeking and that surrender to God's rule alone that God will show us what he has for us, and he will take care of everything else. God is with us for doing his purposes alone. He is not going to help us with something else. He loves us too much. He gives good gifts to his children.

God gives you what you need in order to do what God has called you to do!

"Then the LORD put out his hand and touched my mouth; and the LORD said to me, 'Now I have put my words in your mouth.'" A prophet needs God's words in his or her mouth. God put his words into Jeremiah's mouth because his calling and purpose was to be a prophet. God puts in us what we need in order to do what he calls us to do. What has God been putting into you? That in itself can be some indication of your purpose. What kind of passion do you have in the Lord? What stirs your heart? What God-breathed thing is ready to come forth from you because God put it in you?

The Lord touches us. The Lord put out his hand and touched Jeremiah's mouth. Jeremiah said, "Truly I do not know how to speak." So the Lord touched him at the point of his inadequacy. The Lord will touch us at the point of our weakness and use us from where we are weak, so that he is glorified.

God will take someone who has spent years in the streets and make him a witness of God's power to transform lives. God took Mary Magdalene, who he delivered from seven demons, and made her a witness to his resurrection. God will take someone who spent years in the church, religious but knowing little of God, and make her humbled by God's forgiveness. God took Paul, a man serious about righteousness, and showed him that his righteousness was like filthy rags, and then he made Paul a powerful witness to God's grace. God takes us from wherever we are and frees us for the new thing that he wants to do in and through us.

God has a purpose for each of us. Why should we waste time on anything else? We do not know how many days we may yet have to live out God's purpose for us. Now is the time. Now is the day of salvation. Seek first God's reign and purpose today! Our new life is found in living under God's reign. There is nothing back there in the old life under our own rule. It did nothing for us, and we had no purpose there. We didn't know who we were or why we were here. But now we are discovering our true selves in God's presence. There is no going back!

> If I build up again the very things that I once tore down, then I demonstrate that I am a transgressor. For through the law I died to the law, so that I might live to God. I have been crucified with Christ; and it is no longer I who live, but it is Christ who lives in me. And the life I now live in the flesh I live by faith in the Son of God, who loved me and gave himself for me. (Galatians 2:18-20)

We live by faith now, trusting in God's purposes for us. Our life is now about him, what he has for us and where he is leading us. He has a way for us to serve others that fits who we are as he has created us to be.

In August Wilson's play, *Joe Turner's Come and Gone*, the main character says, "Everyone has a song." Of one person he says, "His song is a binding song." Of another, "His song heals." To another, "You have lost your song." You are bound, having bound yourself up, so that you have forgotten your song!

Have you forgotten your purpose? Are you so bound up that you have forgotten your song? Have you been looking for life in all the wrong places? The Lord says, "Seek me with all your heart and you will surely find me!" We find him and we find our purpose and our way of serving! It is time to know how God wants to use us in the lives of others. Receive from him your ministry and service.

16 Ministry In A Time Of Breakdown

In the year that King Uzziah died, I saw the Lord sitting on a throne, high and lofty; and the hem of his robe filled the temple. Seraphs were in attendance above him; each had six wings: with two they covered their faces, and with two they covered their feet, and with two they flew. And one called to another and said: "Holy, holy, holy is the LORD of hosts; the whole earth is full of his glory." The pivots on the thresholds shook at the voices of those who called, and the house filled with smoke. And I said: "Woe is me! I am lost, for I am a man of unclean lips, and I live among a people of unclean lips; yet my eyes have seen the King, the LORD of hosts!" Then one of the seraphs flew to me, holding a live coal that had been taken from the altar with a pair of tongs. The seraph touched my mouth with it and said: "Now that this has touched your lips, your guilt has departed and your sin is blotted out." Then I heard the voice of the Lord saying, "Whom shall I send, and who will go for us?" And I said, "Here am I; send me!" And he said,

"Go and say to this people:
'Keep listening, but do not comprehend;
    keep looking, but do not understand.'
Make the mind of this people dull,
    and stop their ears,

and shut their eyes,
so that they may not look with their eyes,
and listen with their ears,
and comprehend with their minds,
and turn and be healed."

Then I said, "How long, O Lord?" And he said:

"Until cities lie waste without inhabitant,
and houses without people,
and the land is utterly desolate;
until the LORD sends everyone far away,
and vast is the emptiness in the midst of the
land.
Even if a tenth part remain in it,
it will be burned again,
like a terebinth or an oak
whose stump remains standing
when it is felled."

The holy seed is its stump. (Isaiah 6:1-13)

The time in which Isaiah lived was very similar to our time. Religion was easy, and God was tame. People expected God to be on their side. They might say, "God bless Judah," as easily as many say, "God bless America." Even while people lived distant from God, they talked easily about God. As in our time, there was great social injustice and inequity. The rich were getting richer and the poor were getting poorer.

Therefore the word of the Lord through Isaiah was: "Wash yourselves; make yourselves clean; remove the evil of your doings from before my eyes; cease to do evil, learn to do good; seek justice, rescue the oppressed, defend the orphan, plead for the widow" (Isaiah 1:16-17). God was calling his people back to himself. And then finally, in the sixth chapter of Isaiah, his people being unresponsive to his call, God had his prophet speak a message of judgment. "And he said, 'Go and say to this people: 'Keep listening, but do not comprehend; keep looking, but do not understand.' Make the mind of this people dull, and stop their ears, and shut their eyes, so that they may not look with their eyes, and listen with their ears, and comprehend with their minds, and turn and be healed.'" This people refused God's word for so long that they will no longer be able to hear it. There will be only God's judgment.

"Then I said, 'How long, O Lord?' And he said: 'Until cities lie waste without inhabitant, and houses without people, and the land is utterly desolate; until the LORD sends everyone far away, and vast is the emptiness in the midst of the land. Even if a tenth part remain in it, it will be burned again, like a terebinth or an oak whose stump remains standing when it is felled.' The holy seed is its stump." God will bring judgment! If this was true for Judah, should we expect anything else for these United States of America and for the church in this nation? Paul says that God's judgment comes to the household of God first. Why? Because we have not been the witnesses God called us to be. We have not been the salt, light, yeast our society has needed us to be—largely because we have often acted not much differently from the rest of society. We have made being Christian easy for ourselves. We have broadened the hard, narrow road. We have taken God's grace and cheapened it. Many easily say, "I accept Christ, I accept Christ," while not following him.

God is getting Isaiah ready for his judgment. God is getting him ready to serve others in a time of judgment and breakdown. Are we prepared to serve or minister to others in a time of judgment and breakdown? Are we prepared to be a part of the remnant? God always has a remnant. "The holy seed is the stump." There is a remnant to minister to people in a time of judgment and breakdown.

Judgment comes to bring us down to a place where we will start to look up again. When judgment and breakdown come, people reach out for help. They reach out for God. There needs to be a remnant who are ready to respond to them. God gets us ready to minister and serve in a time of judgment and breakdown.

God prepared Isaiah for ministry in such a time, and he prepares us in the same way: (1) God allows us to experience his holiness and our sinfulness. (2) God forgives and cleanses us. (3) God sends us out.

God allows us to experience his holiness and our sinfulness.

> In the year that King Uzziah died, I saw the Lord sitting on a throne, high and lofty; and the hem of his robe filled the temple. Seraphs were in attendance above him; each had six wings: with two they covered their faces, and with two they covered their feet, and with two they flew. And one called to another and said: "Holy, holy, holy is the LORD of hosts; the whole earth is full of his glory."

God brings us into his presence so that we can know ourselves. True worship often unsettles us because we are brought before the living God and we experience his glory. The whole earth is filled with his glory and God is holy! "Holy, holy, holy is the Lord of hosts!" We experience the distance between us and God and the discrepancy that God is holy and we are sinful. We experience ourselves as lost, broken, unclean and very needy. "Woe is me! I am lost, for I am a man of unclean lips, and I live among a people of unclean lips; yet my eyes have seen the King, the

LORD of hosts!" "It's me, it's me, it's me, O Lord, standing in the need of prayer!" We cannot point the finger at others anymore. We are unable to act like we are the good guys and they—whoever they are—are the bad guys. Who are we to point the finger at someone else? We are lost. We have unclean lips among people of unclean lips. It is no longer them and us. We are all in the same boat.

We cannot share God's message from a point above others. We are among them and one of them. The message God gives to us addresses all of us together. When you and I want to be judgmental and critical of someone else, it is a sign that we need to spend time in the presence of the living God. God will help us to get things back into perspective! As Martin Luther said, "We are all beggars." If we have found some bread, it is not so that we can judge someone who has not, but so that we can share what we have received.

When we spend time in God's presence, we prepare for ministry to others because in his presence we experience his holiness and our sinfulness. Needy people will come to us. People under God's judgment will come to us. They will come to other needy people.

Have you been getting ready for God's judgment and the ministry that comes with it? In a time of judgment and breakdown, people who know they need help—really need help—reach out to people who know from where help comes. Are you letting God prepare you for the work that he has for you? God allows us to experience his holiness, our sinfulness and our deep need for him, so that we do not run anywhere else for help. God alone is our help and our redeemer.

God forgives and cleanses us.

"Then one of the seraphs flew to me, holding a live coal that had been taken from the altar with a pair of tongs. The seraph touched my mouth with it and said: 'Now that this has touched your lips, your guilt has departed and your sin is blotted out.'" We have unclean lips. What comes out of our mouths is not clean. It is not honest. We say things about ourselves and others that are not true. Christians say things that are not true. We who follow the one who is the way, the truth and the life, say things that we learned from the world, the flesh and the devil. We say, "I can't," when the truth is that by the grace of God we can. We say, "I am only human," to excuse our sin when the truth is that in Christ we become truly human as God intended us to be, in order that we might live by faith in God and his power. We say, "The devil made me do it," when the truth is we chose to give into the temptation, even though we knew that in every temptation God gives a way of escape. We say, "I can't live without this thing in my life, or this person," when the truth is we cannot live without God.

We say, "I just don't understand how a person can be like that," when the truth is we are like that. "Therefore you have no excuse, whoever you are, when you judge others; for in passing judgment on another you condemn yourself, because you, the judge, are doing the very same things" (Romans 2:1). We say, "I did the best I could," when the truth is we have no idea what our best is. We are still on a journey. The best is ahead. We say, "I did all I could do," when the truth is only God knows what the all is; we see in a mirror dimly and only know in part. We say, "I just couldn't help myself," when the truth is God could have helped us, and if we had let him, we wouldn't have fallen into the sin we fell into.

We lie and our lips are unclean. We need for God to touch our lips and make them clean. And God comes to do that through Jesus Christ. He touches our lips so that we are forgiven and cleansed. He says to us, "Your guilt has departed and your sin is blotted out." To the woman caught in adultery, Jesus says, "I do not condemn you. Go and sin no more." To the tax collector who repents, he says, "Today salvation has come to this man's house." To the thief on the cross, he says, "Today, you will be with me in paradise." "If we confess our sins, he who is faithful and just will forgive us our sins and cleanse us from all unrighteousness" (1 John 1:9). God forgives and cleanses us.

God sends us out.

"Then I heard the voice of the Lord saying, 'Whom shall I send, and who will go for us?' And I said, 'Here am I; send me!'" The living God does not leave forgiven sinners idle. If we are not doing God's will, we will be doing the devil's will. God has a purpose for our lives. He now has something for us to do. We have been forgiven and cleansed. And we continue to be forgiven and cleansed. We have been delivered from bondage, and we must now rebuild our lives. We have been set free to do something.

Our Lord speaks to our freedom. He speaks to people who, having been set free by the power of God, can now take responsibility. He says, "Whom shall I send, and who will go for us?" He puts it in the form of a question. He calls forth our response of loving gratitude for what he has done. He calls forth from us our free response to his call. There is, of course, nothing else for us to do, but it is important that our response is not a slavish one but rather the free response of a child of God: "Here I am; send me!"

Thank you Lord for forgiving me. Thank you for setting me free. Here I am. Send me!

I had a brother who was with us for three years and then died of leukemia. He was the fifth and youngest child. As a three year old, his favorite phrase was, "Let's do it!" His older siblings or sometimes the entire family would talk about doing something. It did not seem to matter to him what it was. He would break in with, "Let's do it!" God wants to hear our "Let's do it!" "Here am I; send me."

Notice that God asks the question, "Whom shall I send?" and expects an answer before he even tells us what he wants us to do. God does not first tell us what he has for us to do and then ask us if we want to do it. When we thought we were in charge of our lives, we wanted to know in advance what we were being asked to do, and then we would decide whether or not we were going to do it. Not so anymore with the living God. We are to learn to walk by faith, not by sight. Our Lord says to us, "Trust me. Trust me in what I am going to do in your life and with your life." When Isaiah said, "Here am I, send me," he was responding in trust and obedience to the God who had forgiven him.

Jesus came to fishermen by the Sea of Galilee and said to them, "Follow me, and I will make you fish for people" (Matthew 4:19). He gave them no more explanation. They would have to find out as they followed Jesus what he meant by fishing for people. God does the same with us. When God calls us out of our comfort zones, he calls us to step out in faith into new areas. He calls us to turn away from distractions and give ourselves to him. He wants us to say, "Here am I, send me," and then to step out, not knowing all that he will do in and through us in our families, households and relationships. When God calls us into some form of ministry, he does not inform us in advance of everything we will deal with. His call is a call to trust.

God sends us out. We are to be salt, light and yeast in our society and the world. God is sending us as needy people among other needy people in a time of judgment and breakdown in order to witness, serve and build up. So, where has God been taking you, my sister, my brother? Perhaps at this point you say, "God has not been taking me anywhere. Fear has been taking me somewhere. Lusts have been taking me somewhere." Child of God, God knows. And he has the remedy. He comes to touch you with his love, to cleanse and heal you again and to free you more. He comes to raise you up for his purposes in this time of breakdown. He comes to lead you. We can, right now, acknowledge our own sin and brokenness, receive his forgiveness and cleansing and let him now lead us.

17 From "Me First" To Servant

"Do not be afraid, little flock, for it is your Father's good pleasure to give you the kingdom. Sell your possessions, and give alms. Make purses for yourselves that do not wear out, an unfailing treasure in heaven, where no thief comes near and no moth destroys. For where your treasure is, there your heart will be also. Be dressed for action and have your lamps lit; be like those who are waiting for their master to return from the wedding banquet, so that they may open the door for him as soon as he comes and knocks. Blessed are those slaves whom the master finds alert when he comes; truly I tell you, he will fasten his belt and have them sit down to eat, and he will come and serve them. If he comes during the middle of the night, or near dawn, and finds them so, blessed are those slaves." "But know this: if the owner of the house had known at what hour the thief was coming, he would not have let his house be broken into. You also must be ready, for the Son of Man is coming at an unexpected hour." (Luke 12:32-40)

Nearly three dozen public school students have been killed in Chicago so far this year at the time of this writing, most of them shot to death. What we are experiencing in Chicago is being experienced across our land. As (then presidential candidate) Barack Obama pointed out on the south side of Chicago, "From South-Central L.A., to Newark, New Jersey, there's an epidemic of violence that is sickening the soul of this nation." Bob Herbert of the New York Times wrote, "More attention to this crisis of violence is needed, and more police resources, and more jobs, and better schools, and improved prison re-entry programs, and tighter gun controls. But more than anything else, a cultural change is needed."

It is this "more than anything else" that I believe I am called, day in and day out, to focus on: "A cultural change is needed." Or more to the point, the spiritual roots of a cultural change. I think about the parents of children who have killed children. They often say, "I don't know what went wrong." Or, "This is not what I taught my child." What we often fail to see is that it is not always a matter of what we taught, but what we failed to teach, and also what we failed to live throughout our society and culture.

We live in a culture and social condition of hedonism— life oriented to our own pleasure. We learn from this culture that life is all about me, myself and I. This culture of hedonism has spiritual roots in human pride, each of us trying to play god. The temptation that came through the serpent in the Genesis story was, "You shall be like God." You can be the center of your own existence. You can make up your own word. You need not live by any other direction than that of your own desires.

There are, of course, other forces at work beyond individual hedonism. There are forces that make violence a solution and guns readily available, but the spiritual roots of the problem are in life centered in self rather than God. More than anything else, my personal calling is to speak God's good news of spiritual transformation. I am grateful that there are others who are called to address other dimensions of this problem. But I am under call to proclaim that, with God, change is possible, that the me-first mentality can be changed to a servant mentality. God came to us in Jesus who said that he "came not to be served but to serve, and to give his life a ransom for many." In our self-obsessed culture, where we are into self-help big time, God has made himself present in Jesus who gave up his life for our deliverance from this culture of death and our restoration to life.

Jesus is with us right now to serve us! The Greek word for serve in the above text is διαχονε which is often translated *minister* as well as *serve*. I like the word "minister" because it implies giving to someone something they truly need. Ministry does not simply serve a person's desires, which can bring confusion, but it serves the person. Jesus says, "Be dressed for action." Or as the NIV translation has it, "Be dressed ready for service." I like that! Be dressed ready for ministry! Jesus comes to save us out of our "me first" mentality and give us a new mind, the mind of a minister and servant of others.

Jesus dresses us for serving.

Jesus himself gets us ready for serving. Without him we can do nothing. Without him our serving is self-serving. This means that we have to let Jesus minister to us. If we do not let him minister to us, then he will not be able to minister through us. Jesus came into the world to minister, and he ministers to us especially through the word. With his first followers, he got right in their midst and their mess and spoke God's word to them. When they were talking about who was the greatest in the kingdom of God, he shared with them: "The greatest in the kingdom of God is the servant of all." When they could not cast out a particular demon, he gave them instruction: "This demon, in order to be cast out, takes much prayer." When they did not understand the meaning of his parables, he broke it down for them. Jesus constantly ministered to them through the word.

We must let Jesus minister to us through the word, if we are going to minister to others. We must let Jesus speak his word which is living and active, sharper than a two edged sword cutting to the depths of our being. Jesus speaks right to that point in our lives where we have to make a change and trust and take another step. Jesus speaks to us from the heart of the Father, not from our own heart. He speaks to us from the desires of his Father for our lives, not from our own desires. Sometimes we will listen for a word that fits our desires. When we do that we close our spiritual ears to Jesus and open them to our own feelings, attitudes and issues. Our physical ears can tune out sounds in order to hear the sound we want to hear. Our spiritual ears can do something similar, even tuning out the word of Jesus for the words of our own desires.

Jesus knows our feelings, desires, thinking and inner life, but does not speak to us from them. He speaks to us from the heart of the Father. He is not influenced by how we are going to *feel* about his word. I imagine Peter felt really good when, responding to Peter's confession that he was the Messiah, Jesus said, "Flesh and blood has not revealed this to you, but my Father in heaven" (Matthew 16:17). I can see Peter elated! But then Peter said something that sounded good in his own mind but was way off, and Jesus said to him, "Get behind me, Satan" (Matthew 16:23)! I suspect that was a real downer for Peter. But Jesus spoke truth to him and the truth was setting Peter free!

Jesus is dressing us for serving others by ministering to us through his word. My sister, my brother, let Jesus minister to you! He is making you into a minister that he can use to bring healing and deliverance to others.

Jesus dresses us for serving, not for religion.

This is so important for us to see. Jesus does not dress us up for a worship service. Worship, in spirit and in truth, flows forth into ministry to others. Worship, in spirit and in truth, is Jesus dressing us for serving. As we bow down our hearts, surrendering ourselves to the will of the Father, we are being made ready to go back out into the world and minister to others.

God cannot abide worship assemblies that bring no repentance and change to our lives, no faith and obedience to God's word. God gets tired of this kind of religion. Hear the word of the Lord in Isaiah: "I cannot endure solemn assemblies with iniquity. Your new moons and your appointed festivals my soul hates; they have become a burden to me, I am weary of bearing them. When you stretch out your hands, I will hide my eyes from you; even though you make many prayers, I will not listen" (Isaiah 1:13-15). The Lord tells us, through Isaiah, the kind of worship and surrender to his will that he desires: "Learn to do good; seek justice, rescue the oppressed, defend the orphan, plead for the widow" (Isaiah 1:17). These are action words: learn, seek, rescue, defend, plead. We are to be dressed for action and ready to serve. And our worship is to be the bowing down of our hearts and lives so that as we move out from worship, we move into action.

Jesus speaks of serving this way: "Sell your possessions, and give alms." In other words, give with mercy to those in need. Serving involves giving of ourselves and of that which is in our possession. We often get fearful at this point, but Jesus tells us that we are not to be afraid to let go and to give. He says, "Do not be afraid, little flock, for it is your Father's good pleasure to give you the kingdom."

Jesus dresses us for serving, not for religion. Our worship is tested by what we do as we move out from worship, not by how wonderful our prayers sound or how great the singing is. In true worship, Jesus is dressing us for ministry!

Serving means taking orders.

Obedience may be our greatest problem. Being dressed for action means being ready to take orders. Jesus speaks of servants ready to open the door when their master comes knocking. They are alert for his coming, doing what he has given for them to do while he is away. We are to be this way toward Jesus.

The Lord speaking through the prophet Isaiah says, "If you are willing and obedient, you shall eat the good of the land." Here are questions that each of us can ask ourselves: "Is my heart willing and ready to obey, or am I rebellious and ready to refuse?" "Do I vacillate between the two?"

Jesus dresses us to serve in his service. He does not dress us to serve in somebody else's service or in our own service. If you are a soldier, your uniform represents the training you have undergone and the service you are in. As soon as you put on the uniform, you know you will be taking orders. If you are an athlete in a team sport, as soon as you put on your uniform and walk out on the field or the court, you know you are under orders as well. You are going to have to do what the coach tells you to do. The crowd and the fans may have other ideas, but you will have to obey the coach. Jesus is our captain and coach. He is our Lord and Master. We are the servants. Servants do not say, "I will serve, but I will be the master of what, when and where I serve." We are not serving Jesus when we are being the masters of our own serving.

We can serve for all the wrong reasons. We can get involved in service projects in order to not feel guilty. We can do service as a way to keep out of trouble. We say,

"Well, if I am doing this good service, I won't be doing this other thing that I know is wrong and that I keep falling back into." Instead of letting Jesus truly minister to us and get into our mess and uncover our hurt and expose our sin, we try to be our own saviors, filling in the void with our own chosen service projects. We are still playing master. We can be so locked into controlling when, where and how we serve that when our Lord shows up at the door calling for us to let him in, we do not even recognize it is him. We say, "I don't open doors." "I am not ready to do that right now." "Its not mine to do." "Go talk to James or John."

But Jesus still knocks at the door. He wants us to open to him as our master and Lord. Our Lord wants to minister to us. Only he can set us free to serve. "Blessed are those slaves whom the master finds alert when he comes; truly I tell you, he will fasten his belt and have them sit down to eat, and he will come and serve them." The master having the slaves sit down to eat and then dressing himself for action in order to serve them is not the typical master-slave relationship. But it is the way things are done in the kingdom of God. Jesus is Master and Lord because he is servant of all. And he is dressed ready to serve.

Jesus is always present to minister to us through his word. To his followers he says, "Be dressed ready to serve. Be alert for my coming. Be about the things that I give for you to do. Do not get caught up in the worries and lusts of this world. Look to me and be obedient."

Jesus loves to minister to us. He loves to get us dressed for serving. He gets us ready to go to our homes and situations to begin ministering. We have children that need our ministry. We have spouses and people in our households that need our ministry. They do not need our anger, hurt, bitterness or grudges. They need the ministry of our forgiveness. We come to Jesus so that he can heal our hurts and dress us for serving.

Jesus wants to send us back to our homes not so that we can pick up a fight where we left off, or continue badgering and belittling or play out the same scenarios to which we have become accustomed. He wants to heal us of inner hurts. He wants to deliver us from that which has us bound. He wants to save us from our sins, so that we are free to minister to our family and others in his name.

What has been getting in your way today of truly serving and ministering to others in your life? Jesus wants to get at what gets in the way. Is there unforgiveness? Is there bitterness? Are there power struggles and issues of control? Is there pride? Whatever it is, Jesus wants to get at it. He stands at the door and knocks, waiting for us to again let him in that he might minister healing and new life in us.

18 Good Suffering

> I am now rejoicing in my sufferings for your sake, and in my flesh I am completing what is lacking in Christ's afflictions for the sake of his body, that is, the church. (Colossians 1:24)

How and why does Paul rejoice in his sufferings? People generally do not do this, certainly not most people in our society. We spend much time and energy avoiding suffering. When suffering comes, we complain about it. We have all kinds of prescription and non-prescription drugs for alleviating physical pain. And if the pain is emotional, we may try smoking or drinking it away, or use TV as a drug, or sex or violence. If we cannot avoid it, we get on our pity pot, and we find companions in misery.

And yet, suffering is a part of life. No one avoids suffering. We suffer the consequences of our bad decisions. We suffer because of the bad decisions others make. We suffer from accidents and illnesses. We suffer with each other. We suffer in relationships. We suffer from the weather, from floods, drought, and hurricanes. We suffer from government and corporate decisions. We suffer from injustice, racism, greed, general human selfishness, ours and others. We suffer from addictions, obsessions and sins. Paul talks about suffering for the body of Christ!

The word suffer comes from the Latin, *sufferre*—to bear up or endure. In Greek, the word for suffer is παθημα—something undergone, as in hardship or pain. Paul says that he is rejoicing in his sufferings, in his undergoing hardship and pain for the sake of the church. And Paul is not the only one that thinks like this in the New Testament. In Acts chapter 5, after the apostles had been flogged and ordered not to speak of Jesus anymore, it says: "As they left the council, they rejoiced that they were considered worthy to suffer dishonor for the sake of the name." These first followers of Jesus rejoice at suffering for the sake of Jesus and for suffering for the sake of the church which is the body of Jesus!

Why? How? What does this mean for you and me? Suffering is not going to go away. Enduring hardship is not going to vanish. There will be consequences from our sins and the sins of others, as well as from illnesses, accidents, bad weather and bad government. These are not going to go away until Jesus appears. So, I want to know what Paul means when he says he rejoices in suffering, especially when he says he rejoices in his suffering for the sake of the church. And what does he mean that in his flesh he is "completing what is lacking in Christ's afflictions for the sake of his body, that is, the church?" Is there such a thing as "good suffering?"

"All things work together for the good for those who love God and are called according to his purposes"— apparently even bad things that happen to us, even suffering. God took the cross, the emblem of suffering and shame and made it the way of salvation and victory. Good Friday is about good suffering!

Suffering for the sake of our calling.

Paul suffered for the sake of his calling.

> I became [the church's] servant according to God's commission that was given to me for you, to make the word of God fully known, the mystery that has

been hidden throughout the ages and generations but has now been revealed to his saints. To them God chose to make known how great among the Gentiles are the riches of the glory of this mystery, which is Christ in you, the hope of glory. It is he whom we proclaim, warning everyone and teaching everyone in all wisdom, so that we may present everyone mature in Christ. (Colossians 1:25-28)

Paul was called and commissioned by God to make God's word known. Paul endured hardship for the sake of his commission. What God had commissioned him to do, he would carry out to the end. He let us know some of what he had endured for the sake of sharing the word of God with others:

Five times I have received from the Jews the forty lashes minus one. Three times I was beaten with rods. Once I received a stoning. Three times I was shipwrecked; for a night and a day I was adrift at sea; on frequent journeys, in danger from rivers, danger from bandits, danger from my own people, danger from Gentiles, danger in the city, danger in the wilderness, danger at sea, danger from false brothers and sisters; in toil and hardship, through many a sleepless night, hungry and thirsty, often without food, cold and naked. And, besides other things, I am under daily pressure because of my anxiety for all the churches. (2 Corinthians 11)

Now none of us has exactly the same calling as Paul, and we are unlikely to endure the kinds of things he did. Nevertheless, all of us have a calling to share Christ with others. And all of us will have to endure something in order to share Christ with others—whether it is a matter of door-to-door evangelism, ministry to our children and family, sharing with friends and acquaintances, visiting and praying with someone in the hospital, walking with someone on the road to recovery from addiction, or attending to someone who is ill. These ministries are part of the normal Christian life. Enduring trials for the sake of others with the help of the Holy Spirit is part of the normal Christian life. Suffering hardship for the sake of Christ's body is part of the normal Christian life.

Undergoing suffering for the sake of others starts in our homes and moves out from there. When we get up in the middle of the night to respond to the cries of a child, we endure the lack of sleep for the sake of our child. When we give guidance to our teens with grace and mercy while keeping it real, we may at times endure their rolling eyes—and do so without judging them or putting them down. When we respond to the concerns of our spouse and endure struggles in our relationships, we grow in grace through endurance. We undergo struggle and hardship when we deal with the issues in our household, rather than "sweep them under the rug." We suffer attitudes on our job and bear with them so that we may continue to welcome others with the welcome of Christ. We endure the behavior problems of children in order to keep ministering to them. In all this, the Holy Spirit helps us to endure and press on for the sake of a hurting world.

Now I know we must move step by step. In the beginning of our Christian walk, we need much receiving from others and nurture in Christ. But there comes a time when our receiving moves into being sent. I enjoyed my children when they were two or three years of age, but I did not want them to grow up to be ten years of age and still be acting like they were three. I wanted them to grow to be mature adults moving out on their own and taking responsibility for their own lives. This is true for growth in Christian maturity as well. At some point, everyone of us must let God send us out to serve and share the good news with others. We must do so with the gifts God has given us in response to his call. And we will have to take up our cross and follow Jesus.

When Paul speaks of suffering for the sake of Christ's body, he is talking about the cross that is attached to every calling. If you are living out your calling today, you are carrying a cross. You are enduring for the sake of others. And this is the normal Christian life. You are suffering loss. Paul writes of suffering the loss of all things: "For his sake, I have suffered the loss of all things, and I regard them as rubbish, in order that I may gain Christ." You are suffering the loss of your agendas and plans, your comfort, convenience and ease, and your controlling ways.

The world needs a church and followers of Jesus who will suffer loss for the sake of sharing God's love with the world. I do not know how much the world needs "prosperity religion." It already has its own brand of that. It does not need more Christians talking about how God has blessed them. It needs more Christians willing to suffer for the sake of sharing the good news of Jesus Christ with others, even when the going gets hard and then harder.

Jesus told us that we each have a cross. It goes with our calling, and we are not to run from it but take it up and carry it. Let us not fight our cross. My sister, my brother, it goes with our calling. Jesus says to us, "If any want to become my followers, let them deny themselves and take up their cross daily and follow me" (Matthew 16:24). We gain by suffering loss. We gain by enduring. We gain our lives. Jesus says, "For those who want to save their life will lose it, and those who lose their life for my sake, and for the sake of the gospel, will save it" (Mark 8:35). With endurance, we gain purpose, commitment, a future with hope and above all, the surpassing value of knowing Christ Jesus as Lord.

Suffering in Christ.

By his sufferings Paul says he is completing what is lacking in Christ's afflictions. This is a strange statement, given that Paul elsewhere, as does the entire New Testament, makes clear that nothing can be added to Christ's cross. What God accomplished through Jesus Christ's dying and rising is complete. It is not lacking, at least when it comes to our salvation. Paul must mean something else here.

The Christ who suffered on the cross for us entered into our suffering and enters into it today in our lives. And he does so through his body. By his stripes, we continue to be healed. By the stripes of his body, the church, by our losing our lives for his sake and the gospel, by our entering into the hurts and burdens and brokenness of others, Christ is bringing healing. What is lacking in Christ's afflictions? Christians willingly entering into the hurts, burdens and afflictions of those that are sent into their lives. We complete what is lacking in Christ's afflictions, when we enter into the afflictions of others, no longer running from the needs around us but taking up our cross and ministering to others in the way God has called us.

Jesus expected his followers to follow him all the way to Jerusalem where he would suffer and die and to remain with him through it all. When he called Peter, James and John to pray with him in the Garden of Gethsemane, he was calling them to suffer with him, to walk with him through the ordeal, to be with him. He never said, "You don't have to go to Jerusalem with me. You don't have to be my witnesses when I am on trial. You do not have to share my agony." It grieved Jesus when Peter denied him, even though he knew Peter would. Sometimes

Jesus' followers had to encourage one another. When Jesus turned toward Jerusalem, Thomas said, "Let us go and die with him." They understood.

In Acts, when followers were jailed or beaten, they came together in prayer meetings and rejoiced that they could suffer for the name, and they prayed until power came down. Then they went out to share the word again, entering into a broken and hostile world to witness for the sake of the world. They continued to encourage one another in the Lord: "Consider him who endured such hostility against himself from sinners, so that you may not grow weary or lose heart. In your struggle against sin you have not yet resisted to the point of shedding your blood....Therefore lift your drooping hands and strengthen your weak knees, and make straight paths for your feet, so that what is lame may not be put out of joint, but rather be healed" (Hebrews 12).

They were encouraged to fight the good fight and to be faithful to the end. I believe it is no different for us. God is calling the church to recover what we have lost in our love for Jesus and be willing to endure for the sake of his body. We see what is happening in our world, and we cannot walk on the other side anymore. We see what is happening to our children. We are being called to complete what is lacking in Christ's afflictions by entering into the afflictions of others, walking with them, sharing the love of Christ with them, and trusting in the Holy Spirit to help us.

Paul rejoices in being able to share with Christ in suffering for the sake of Christ's body. We do that with those we love. If I have to go through something for the sake of my wife, that she may be helped or protected or cared for or kept from harm, I will suffer all kinds of hardship, and even life itself if it means life for her. I say that from a relationship of love. Paul is writing out of a love relationship.

Are you living in this kind of relationship with Jesus today? That is what he has for us! A love relationship that calls forth our enduring hardship for his sake and for the sake of his body. Jesus has given us something worth living for because its worth dying for. The truth is we are going to suffer in this world. I'd rather do it for Jesus than because I have chosen a broad, easy road that leads to destruction.

Perhaps you are facing hardship today. You know what God is calling you to do and you see hardship ahead. You have a difficult step to take. You are going to endure struggle and adversity if you take it. But it is a step of love because God calls you through the needs of your neighbor who is hurting. My brother, my sister, God is with you to bear you up. "All things work to the good for those who love God and are called according to his purposes." There is life in suffering for his name and for the sake of others. This is good suffering, and is part of the normal Christian life.

Conclusion

We have been released from bondage to rebuild our lives. We have been set free and are in the process of being set free from false attachments and dependencies, so that we might now rebuild. And we are given the tools for rebuilding in the Word and Spirit of God. We are not left without direction and power.

God has provided what is necessary for our release and our rebuilding. He has come to us in Jesus Christ who died for us and was raised for us and through whom we are set free and formed into a body. In that body, that fellowship, we are nurtured, encouraged, challenged and empowered. It is in the community of God's people that we find the building blocks for the new life into which we have been born.

In the body of Christ, there are gifts and ministries. We receive a share in those gifts and are given ministries that fit who God created and redeemed us to be. Above all, there is the Word and Spirit of God by which we receive continued deliverance and healing, and by which we are sustained for the journey.

We are on a journey. It is a journey of faith. We have steps to take. At first, those steps are those of needy people receiving the nourishment of the word and the fellowship. Increasingly those steps also become steps with purpose as we discover how God is calling us to use our time, talent and possessions. We remain needy, but we are daily experiencing from God what we need for the journey, and we are growing in our sense of who we are and what we are about.

Initially, our homes are our places of ministry and service, but as we grow, we move increasingly outward to a hurting and broken world. We are discovering that God sends us out to bring his good news in word and deed. We may share the good news with others on the street or on our job, in our schools and in our neighborhoods, in hospitals and nursing homes. We make ourselves available to respond to the needs of others—to those who are hungry and homeless, as well as those who, by worldly standards, are successful but nevertheless empty. We find that they, like us, have idolatries and obsessions, addictions and false attachments, and they need to be set free. We share the good news: "If the Son makes you free, you will be free indeed."

In all this, we must endure suffering. We suffer with our own brokenness and the hurts of others. Not everyone receives the word or receives us. There is rejection, misunderstanding, inconveniences and confrontations. There are long hours ministering to hurting people who often react out of their hurts. There are nights with little sleep. There are hours of prayer for others. There is daily dying to desires in order to do what our Father in heaven has for us and which in the end is the very thing that fits us and fulfills us. All these things are working for our good and building us up.

We endure with a purpose. We have something to do today that has to do with our true selves as God has created us. God is taking us out of our self-absorbed ways. We are growing in seeing others and their needs. We are seeing the environment and context of their needs, and we find ourselves seeking to address a society that is broken and unjust. We are to be salt, light, yeast in this world. We are to speak to the world of what is on the heart of our

Father in heaven for the human creatures he has called forth.

Our lives are being rebuilt. We are becoming builders by God's grace for the transformation of our homes and families, our community and the world. Thanks be to God.